ALL FOR JESUS, BOB

BOB

A Story of Radical Transformation

From the Author of the 10-Week Bible Study
Trees of Righteousness: Living and Lasting Evidence of God

Laura J. Wells

All for Jesus, Bob

ChristTown Ministries, Inc.

Changing Lives By Christ Centered Living

Copyright © 2022, 2023 Laura J. Wells.
ISBN: 979-8-9864945-4-8

All Rights Reserved

No part of this book may be used or reproduced by any means, graphic, electronic, or mechanical, including photocopying, recording, taping or by any information storage retrieval system without the written permission of the author except in the case of brief quotations embodied in critical articles and reviews.

ChristTown Ministries Publishing books may be ordered through Amazon or by contacting:

ChristTown Ministries Publishing
PO Box 417
Quincy, FL 32353
www.ChristTown.org
850-545-7351

Because of the dynamic nature of the Internet, any web addresses or links contained in this book may have changed since publication and may no longer be valid. The views expressed in this work are solely those of the author.

Photos and imagery included herein have been used with the approval of the subjects.

Cover Photo: Bob Wells praising God on Lake Talquin in Florida.
Photo Credit: Taken by his wife Laura on an evening prayer walk.

All for Jesus, Bob

All for Jesus, Bob

From: bob wells bobwells77@gmail.com
To: "laurawells7@gmail.com"
Sent: Monday, February 1, 2010 at 12:04:18 PM CST

My Dearest Angel,

I want you to know I love you heart & soul, and there is no doubt in my mind that He has anointed you for this journey. He didn't give you all of this (love, word & insight) to sit on it! Keep lifting Him up and He will draw all people to Himself.

Everytime I read these words, I am overcome with emotion, tears of joy, and a heart full of gratitude of where God has brought us from. As the old song says, "What He's done for others, He'll do for you."

What He has done for us, He will do for many more. And you, my dear, can be a tool in His hand to lead them to that place. I can never express how blessed I am to have you in my life, the thrill of serving our Savior together, and we have what so many spend a lifetime looking for.

You are "surrounded by a great cloud of witnesses cheering you on!" I'm the one hanging on the fence yelling go, baby, go! :-)

Your time is NOW!

Enjoy the journey . . . NO TURNING BACK!

forever yours, bob

All for Jesus, Bob

Dedication

This book is dedicated to all who have been a part of ChristTown Ministries, Inc. and all those who will be. May our story bless you and give you hope. If Bob and I could have such an amazing transformation in Christ, so can you!

To **Martha Ann**, thank you for saying, "I'm going with you." Your selflessness and giving heart have left an indelible impression on hundreds of hearts—I have told you many times and am saying it again—I don't know where I'd be without you.

Joshua and Jackie Lee, my joy and my heart. Thank you for being willing and obedient to the call. Your dedication and willingness to love and serve what society deems unlovely have profoundly impacted many souls. To God be the glory! May you continue to be His delight!

Most importantly, this work is dedicated to **Jesus Christ**—the One Who forever changed me.
Let Your glory and majesty be magnified!

All for Jesus, Bob

Acknowledgments

Susan Young! My forever friend! Thank you for being the person who asks questions at luncheons like, "If money weren't an issue or object, what would you do?"

You know my answer was I would write Bible Studies and here we are—book number two! Thank you for the countless hours of interviewing me to draw this story out of me, for editing, and for being willing to ask me the hard questions to make the finished product worthy of print. Thank you for being very authentic with me and giving me strong words of correction when needed. For example, when we were at lunch at the beach in Destin, you said to me, "How dare you! How dare you have such incredible gifts and insights and not share them with the world!" This startling truth shifted my perspective from thinking that I had nothing to offer and that people wouldn't be interested in what I had to say to thinking that maybe they would. Your challenge prompted me to start writing.

Thank you for spending countless hours formatting and publishing this book for Amazon. Thank you for loving me and seeing me with the eyes that you do. Without the enthusiasm, encouragement, time, and love you have poured into me and this project, it would never have been completed. Words cannot adequately express the love and gratitude in my heart for you.

Mary Johnson, I appreciate you taking the time to use the incredible mind and eye for detail God has given you to edit the pages of this manuscript. Thank you.

All for Jesus, Bob

Contents

Dedication vi
Acknowledgments viii
Prologue 1
Chapter 1—Looking for Love in All the Wrong Places 7
Chapter 2—Staying Married 17
Chapter 3—Out Of The Pit 29
Chapter 4—Serving & Being Rebuilt 43
Chapter 5—Changing Locks 55
Chapter 6—Ministry of Reconciliation 67
Chapter 7—Life In His Name 79
Chapter 8—Choosing Joy 101
Chapter 9—Walking Through 121
Chapter 10—All For Jesus, Bob 135
About the Author 151
Bibliography 153

ALL FOR JESUS, BOB

A Story of Radical Transformation

All for Jesus, Bob

Prologue

During my early years, I did not always have positive relationships with males. My first kiss happened in the seventh grade and an unpleasant physical encounter with one of my older brother's friends in the eighth grade. The first kiss was sweet and wonderful, the physical encounter was terrifying and life-altering. My father was an incredible man who loved his children and worked hard to raise us the right way. He worked three jobs and was rarely home. When he was home, our interaction was mostly of the disciplinary kind or barely any. I don't remember him to be very affectionate. Words he often spoke are burned into my heart, "I put a roof over your head, clothes on your back, and food on your table. I've done my job."

I understand now that these experiences were the catalyst that sent me on an endless pursuit of being validated and loved by my distorted view of the approval and affection of others, particularly men. I spent too much time looking for love in all the wrong places and too many faces.

Laura's First Marriage

When I got married the first time, I knew I shouldn't have but unfortunately decided to do it anyway. I was in tenth grade the day I first saw him. I hadn't even met or talked to him that day, but I told my sister, "I just saw the man I am going to marry!"

Fast forward four years. I was now engaged to that man, and the wedding invitations were completed and ready to be mailed. I'm at the post office with my sister, sitting in my car next to the mailbox for quite some time, sipping beers. She read my thoughts accurately and said, "You don't have to put those invitations in the box. You don't have to do this if you don't want to." I thought for a moment, "She's right. I don't."

I'm not sure what my response to her was exactly. All I know is that I put the invitations in the box. I was getting married—no turning back now.

> *There's a way of life that looks harmless enough;*
> *look again—it leads straight to hell.*
> *Sure, those people appear to be having a good time,*
> *but all that laughter will end in heartbreak.*
> **Proverbs 14:12-13 MSG**

At the time, I felt I was too far in and couldn't turn back; after all, this was just probably pre-wedding jitters. Somewhere deep inside, I had an inkling not to go through with this marriage, but I did. It seemed right at the time. I was concerned about hurting people by calling it off, and in the end, I ended up hurting many people deeply.

Today, I would say that it was the voice of God giving me that inkling, but I didn't recognize His voice at that time. We were married less than a year before we separated. We were separated for about a year when we got back together and tried again, only for it to end with him standing in the hallway of our apartment telling me he was "sick and tired of trying to make me happy." Those words devastated me and reinforced the feeling that I was unworthy of any man's love and approval, not worth the effort or sacrifice.

> *If you go the wrong way—to the right or to the left—you will hear a voice behind you. It will say, "This is the right way. You should go this way."*
> **Isaiah 30:21 ICB**

Oh, that I would have heeded that voice trying to lead me to go the right way! If my ex-husband or those I hurt by my actions ever read this book, I pray they hear my heart when I say, "I am sorry. So very sorry." As my father would say, "it takes two to tango." I feel in my heart that the failure of the marriage was primarily due to my desire to be loved and the pressure I placed on him to do what only God could for me.

*For He satisfies the longing soul and
fills the hungry soul with goodness.*
Psalm 107:9 NKJV

Not long after my first husband told me he was miserable trying to keep me happy, Bob Wells entered my life. Bob, at the time, was already divorced and had been for a few years.

Bob's First Marriage

If Bob were here to help write this book, he would acknowledge his faults in the failure of the marriage. His first wife was his high school sweetheart. Their romance resulted in her becoming pregnant and then doing the right thing—getting married. He was nineteen years old at the time, and I believe she was just eighteen. He has two boys from his first marriage, Dustin and John. He loved his family, but being such a young father and husband, the weight of the responsibility made him feel trapped.

All for Jesus, Bob

To feel free, he started going to bars and playing pool with his friends after work. He didn't start drinking until he was in his early twenties. With alcoholism in his family, it didn't take long for a drink and a game of pool to turn into several drinks and games and getting home later and later. His absence from home and presence on the enemies' playground resulted in a miserable marriage and ultimately a divorce.

I can't say I know when he started adding drugs to his partying days, but I can say with certainty that he would tell us it started as fun, and his late nights would turn into days of binging. His life unraveled when he began using drugs and he soon became enslaved to drugs and alcohol. It was no longer any fun, and the pleasure and sense of relief had disappeared. As he would put it, "I started doing drugs, and then drugs started doing me." The book of Hebrews clarifies this for us, when speaking of Moses, it says:

> *He chose not to enjoy sin's pleasures.*
> *They only last for a short time.*
> **Hebrews 11:25(b) NIRV**

All for Jesus, Bob

Chapter 1—Looking for Love in All the Wrong Places

What man desires most is unfailing love.
Proverbs 19:22 NIV

I met Bob in a bar—the Silver Slipper in Tallahassee, Florida. Not exactly the opening sentence you would expect in a book titled, **All for Jesus**!

It was a Wednesday night, and we were both attending a professional Builders Association Meeting. Truthfully, the meeting was happening in the banquet room, and we were in the bar.

The first place I ever laid eyes on Bob was at a Village Inn, having an early morning breakfast with some friends after an evening of partying. He was severely intoxicated but managed to slur out these words to me, "Hey baby, you want to go home with me?"

I remember kidding with my friends at the table, "He's really good-looking. Too bad he can't talk!" We continued with our breakfasts without being introduced.

However, one of my friends knew one of the friends sitting at his table.

After some inquiries through mutual acquaintances, I discovered that they called him the 'Mayor of Beachton.' Beachton is a little unincorporated area in South Georgia. I was continually on the lookout for this 'Mayor.' I even drove there to see if I could "run into him." I later discovered that they didn't even have a Mayor!

Let's get back to the bar, the Silver Slipper. It was a Wednesday evening in October of 1987. I was seated at a table in the bar with several friends when Bob walked in. The gentleman sitting next to me, Steve, hollered a friendly greeting to him. I grabbed Steve's necktie, pulled him toward me, and asked, "You know that guy?"

"Yes, I know that guy," he said. "I want to know that guy!" I said, and Steve introduced us. There was an immediate and what would become a lasting attraction.

Bob got my number that evening and called me the next day. He was single; I was still married, about to be divorced. His first invitation was a weekend getaway. BOLD move! I told him no, I couldn't go. I was still married and living with my husband—right? I was married, in a bar, meeting other men, when I told Bob it would be three weeks before I could move out and into the new home we were having built before I would feel comfortable going out with another man.

Talk about stress factors, going through a divorce, building a home, and a full-time career. Even with all that going on, I knew I would go out with him if he called me back. And call back he did! Three weeks to the day! He told me later that his thought was that he would give me one more try. If I said no again, he wouldn't bother with me anymore. We were inseparable from our first date, except for when he would disappear for several days. More on that later . . .

We were on our second date (yep, at another bar) when I asked Bob if he used drugs. He denied being a user, and I believed him. I was okay with drinking at the time. After all, I enjoyed partying too! However, I made it clear to him that I did not want to be involved in any way with drugs.

While on this second date, we also discussed the subject of marriage and children. He specifically told me, "I am never getting married again and never having more children." Understandable! The divorce was hard on him and his family. Again, I made my intentions clear, "Well, I am looking for a husband, and I want to have children! So, I guess we will hang out for a little while and see what happens."

All for Jesus, Bob

Our dating relationship was passionate and stormy. Our arguments were alcohol-related, and undoubtedly, drugs played a part too. We were inseparable unless Bob did one of his disappearing acts. I would not know where he was or what he was doing for several days. His disappearance from my life would make me very upset. My emotions ranged from worry to fury. I never knew if he was hurt, dead, or with another woman. But he was very charming and romantic and could always smooth-talk his way back into my life! (As I write, my heart swells with the intense love we shared. How I miss him.)

We had been dating for three and a half years when Bob and I met for lunch at a little Celebrity Ham store. I had just been to see a doctor regarding issues that I was having with my cervix. We were sitting at a table outside on the patio, discussing what the doctor had told me. She said that if I wanted to have children, I should do it sooner than later because it would not be long before I may not be able to have any at all. As I shared this news, I also told him that if he were serious about not wanting to get married again and have more children, I would be moving on to find someone who would want to marry me and have children. (He always teased that this was when I proposed to him.) Sunday morning, I woke up with a card containing an engagement ring on my nightstand. He had signed the card with these words, "Will you marry me?"

I said, "Yes!"

Bob had a personal relationship with Jesus at the time, and I didn't. He was raised in the Baptist Church, and I in the Catholic Church. Even though we varied in our upbringing, we agreed that the principles of the church were the best way to raise children. We were very aware that not practicing our faith played a big part in our first marriages failing. We wanted Jesus at our wedding, in our marriage, and in our home. We wanted to raise our children with the same moral, ethical, and biblical background that we were blessed to be raised in, so we set out to find a church home and someone of the faith to marry us.

Dedicate your children to God and point them in the way that they should go, and the values they've learned from you will be with them for life.
Proverbs 22:6 TPT

Though one may be overpowered by another, two can withstand him. And a threefold cord is not quickly broken.
Ecclesiastes 4:12 NKJV

So, off to church we went! We visited Catholic, Baptist, and Lutheran churches. We settled in at a little Baptist church in Tallahassee, Florida, called Victory Baptist Church. Bob and his family had attended this church when he was much younger, and he knew the Pastor and his family at this church. We faithfully attended Sunday morning, Sunday night, and Wednesday night services. A friend of his family recommended a Lutheran minister who agreed to marry us if we attended their catechism classes—a several-week course. We agreed and didn't miss a class! Each Sunday morning, until it was completed, we would leave the Lutheran catechism class and travel to Victory Baptist for the Sunday morning service.

All for Jesus, Bob

Interestingly, at the same time, we were going to counseling for the problems in our relationship caused by his drinking. I was fortunate to have six sessions covered at no expense for us through my employment. At our final session with the counselor, I was advised to break off the engagement! Showing me the Jellinek Curve and the stage Bob was in, and what was sure to come, she said, "Find out what direction Bob is going and go as fast and as far as you can in the opposite direction! He is headed for the bottom, where he could die in his addiction, or at best, your life would be complete chaos."

Getting into the car with him after that session, he asked, "What did she say?" I repeated what she said. "What are you going to do?" "I am going to marry you. I love you, Bob. I guess your drinking will be the make or break of our marriage."

On September 1, 1990, we were married. That day a similar thing happened as it did on the day of my first marriage. On both days, I sat in my wedding dress, hair done, nails done, make-up done, anticipating the moment it was time to walk down the aisle. At my first wedding, I fought the urge to run, working hard to convince myself it was just normal wedding day jitters. My dad walked up to me and asked, "Are you OK?" I truly don't know how I responded. He handed me a half of one of his valiums and said, "Take this. It will calm your nerves." I did, and a few minutes later, I floated down the aisle on his arm. The rest of the evening is a blur. The day I married Bob, I had complete peace. While we were waiting for the moment to come, my sister asked, "Are you sure you want to do this?" I looked up at her and said, "I have never been surer of anything."

No matter what the counselor said or what people thought of our future, I knew that Bob loved me, and I loved him. Our love transcended all our issues. Even with his worst traits, he made me feel safe, cared for, loved, and treasured. I believed that I had finally found what I had been looking for—unfailing love—this couldn't have been further from the truth!

Better to dwell in a corner of a housetop, Than in a house shared with a contentious woman.
Proverbs 21:9 NKJV

Bob's drinking and drug use progressed and our lives became more and more unmanageable and chaotic. I certainly was no angel! Proverbs 21:9 was embarrassingly true about me, especially when he would disappear on me for a few days. My anger would flare up and I was not a nice person. I would shout at him, "I am done! We are through!" I would then go into the silent treatment mode, giving you 'looks that can kill' mode. My behavior was very passive-aggressive. I would threaten to leave him if he ever drank and left me alone again. They call this re-drawing the line, which I did too many times. He would fight tooth and nail to keep us together, promising me a better future, that he wouldn't do that again, and I believed he could and would change. He repeatedly re-drew the lines and our situation worsened.

> *The Lord has appeared of old to me, saying:*
> *"Yes, I have loved you with an everlasting love;*
> *Therefore, with loving kindness I have drawn you.*
> **Jeremiah 31:3 NKJV**

God's grace, mercy, and loving kindness continued to draw us to church even through the madness! I was thirty years old and pregnant with Joshua when I had what I like to call a life-changing experience. That little church we were going to gave me a Bible, which I brought to each service and used as the Pastor preached. This was a new concept for me, bringing a Bible to church and reading straight from it.

Initially, I was very skeptical as I listened to Pastor Sanders preach. He talked about being saved and born again, foreign, and unfamiliar terms to me. With each passing service, I became captivated by the Word of God. Pastor Sanders could show us Jesus in every Scripture on which he spoke. My heart quickly came under the Holy Spirit's conviction, and I wanted to be sure I was His and going to Heaven! I would ask Bob questions like, "I did my first confession and communion when I was in grade school; does this mean I am saved?" or "I was confirmed when I was in the eighth grade; does this mean I am saved?" For each question, he would respond, "When it happens, Laura, you will know."

He was so right! There came a day when I surrendered to the drawing of the Holy Spirit. Thirty years old, sitting in my white Cougar at a red light just coming off of I-10 waiting to turn left onto Thomasville Rd., I cried out to Jesus to save me. My soul flooded with His peace—peace like I had never known or felt before. I have never been the same since! I was unaware at the time, but today I know that I had finally met the man that filled my heart with everything it longed for—unconditional love. This love was so consuming and complete that there was no more need for me to be looking for love in all the wrong places!

Chapter 2—Staying Married

And if you are married, stay married.
This is the Master's command, not mine.
1 Corinthians 7:10 MSG

Living with an addicted husband had a detrimental effect on my life. The atmosphere in our home was filled with loneliness and fear. The constant turmoil and desire to have the turmoil removed were ever-present on my mind. Negative emotions emerge whenever I reminisce about these times. The deep-seated fears and loneliness attempt to inundate my soul and steal the peace I enjoy now.

I was more fortunate than others I knew who had the same issue in their homes. Bob would go off on a drinking and drugging binge, leaving me alone for several days at a time. He would vanish from my life. I was torn up inside, not knowing if he was with another woman, seriously injured and in the hospital, dead in a ditch, or had decided he was done with me and wouldn't return. I believe I held it together fairly well on the outside . . . at least at work, church, and socially.

It is better to dwell in a corner of a housetop, than in a house shared with a contentious woman.
Proverbs 25:24 NKJV

I know this is the second time we have seen the above words! These words are found in two different places in the Bible, and I am led to re-state—I was that contentious woman! Anxiety and fear flooded my insides, filling my heart with anger, disappointment, and a feeling of worthlessness. I did not have the tools I do today to help me navigate my anger properly, so when Bob did show back up, let's just say it wasn't pretty. My reactions would sway between being openly aggressive and passively aggressive. When aggressive, my words were loud, hurtful, and full of threats that I never carried out. I used my anger to try to control his behavior—it didn't work!

…for the wrath of man does not produce the righteousness of God.
James 1:20 NKJV

All for Jesus, Bob

Towards the end of Bob's drug use, he would often be sick with flu-like symptoms and sinus headaches. I was unaware of the symptoms of withdrawal and found myself carrying him to doctor after doctor, ER after ER, the whole time worrying that something was wrong with him and missing work to boot! I now know he was doing whatever he could to get pain medications. He, at one point, fell out in a seizure in the kitchen, so I called 911. When the ambulance came, to my surprise, he refused treatment. I later found out he had had a cocaine-induced seizure and didn't want blood work done for fear of the truth coming out! Madness! Insanity! What a time of stress, worry, and pain. Life was completely chaotic and out of control, for both of us.

Another thing you'll notice in an addict's home is the lack of truth. Meaning, it is full of lies. The addict will tell one lie upon another lie to hide their behavior or cover their tracks. To the addict, avoiding the truth is to avoid being found out and reaping any negative consequences for their actions. The result of all the lying is a lack of trust. If you don't have trust in a relationship, in my personal opinion, nothing is right. No relationship can survive under the heavy weight of no trust. Lack of trust progresses to a lack of respect.

So again I say, each man must love his wife as he loves himself, and the wife must respect her husband.
Ephesians 5:33 NLT

Bob and I clearly did not reflect what Ephesians 5:33 NLT says. He was not loving me as he was himself because he was living very selfishly. Everything was about him and how he could get his next high. Because of these circumstances, I lacked the respect for him that the Bible says I should have. Without trust and respect, our relationship began to crumble.

He chose to be mistreated with God's people instead of having the good time that sin could bring for a little while.
Hebrews 11:25 CEV

Bob's lifestyle was fast and furious—all the time. His motto was "whole hog or none at all!" Whenever he dove into something, it was all the way. When he first started drinking, he would tell you he was seeking pleasure. It was a source of enjoyment that brought relief from the pressures of being a newly married young father. His choice was beer and the pool hall instead of the responsibilities waiting for him at home.

If he were here, he would tell you, "I've went fast and furious after it all. I tried fast cars, women, money, alcohol, and drugs. None of these satisfied me, and none of them brought the joy and pleasure I deeply desired. Sure, it was pleasurable for a moment, but Scripture bore true in my life. I wasn't living. I was dying."

> *There is a way that seems right to a man,*
> *But its end is the way of death.*
> **Proverbs 16:25 NKJV**

The pleasure soon wore off, and he started seeking other methods beyond drinking to bring him the pleasure he was seeking—marijuana, cocaine, and ultimately using Dilaudid via a needle.

Bob's usage became more regular; he could not work, so he sold drugs to support his habits. He was completely unreliable and undependable, and those temporary pleasures consumed his life.

Meanwhile, I threw myself at work. Bob was not contributing to the household income and the bills needed to be paid. We needed food and clothing. The struggle, stoic decision, and resolve to leave my problems out of my work and social life are etched vividly in my memory. As I spent long, hard hours striving to succeed, I worried about Bob and wondered what he was up to. I continually had a nagging fear that something was wrong and an obsessive need to be sure he wasn't drinking. In my insanity, I would spend hours trying to find him (although I don't know what I would have done if I did!), which caused me to bring work home and spend time doing it deep into the night after putting Josh to bed. I know now there was nothing I could do to get him to stop drinking and drugging. He had to do that on his own . . .

His addictions progressively worsened over the years. He used to say, "I started doing drugs, and then they started doing me." He found himself in a place where he was powerless, out of control, and about to lose another family.

The thief does not come except to steal, and to kill, and to destroy. I have come that they may have life, and that they may have it more abundantly.
John 10:10 NKJV

Bob lived under the theory, 'all this and Heaven too' for quite some time. He knew he belonged to Jesus and would be with Him in heaven when he died. Bob also knew he was not living the way Jesus would want him to. As his addiction worsened, he realized that living the way he was living was not the joy-filled abundant life Jesus died to give him. His selfishness and the bad choices that the drug usage induced started to catch up to him. He would spend time at the altar in the church, having many conversations with God about his behaviors, troubles, and lack of control. He had a huge hole in his soul that he was attempting to fill with everything except the only thing that truly satisfies . . .

> *For He satisfies the longing soul*
> *And fills the hungry soul with goodness.*
> **Psalm 107:9 NKJV**

Eventually, my eyes were opened to the evident usage of drugs in our home. One morning as I was preparing to go to work (while Bob was laid out in the bed), I came across a gallon baggie half full of a white substance in a drawer on his side of our bathroom cabinet. I roused him up and asked, "What is this?" His response was, "It's boric acid."

I said, "Good, then you won't mind me doing this with it then," and I walked over to the toilet and flushed it. This moment was a life-altering moment for us. I was now faced with the horrible truth. No more denying it. My husband had a serious drug problem. Unbeknownst to me, I had also given him a huge financial problem. That very day, after I was sure that he was gone, I went home, packed a bag for myself and Joshua, and went and stayed with my sister. I avoided him for a couple of days, but I eventually answered his call and agreed to meet with him.

We met at a little lake near downtown Tallahassee. Sitting on a picnic table, he told me about his friend Curtis, who was then clean and sober for two months.

Making promises to go to meetings with Curtis, get help, and change his lifestyle, I agreed to return home.

He began using again within a short period of time, exhibiting all the signs and symptoms of relapse. I was devastated and started making plans to divorce him. What a heartbreaking time! Marriage number two was disintegrating, and truthfully, that was the last thing I wanted! I loved Bob! Praise and glory belong to our awesome God that His kindness and compassion kept us faithful church attenders during these struggles! In the church house, time and time again, I would hear *"stay married"* whisper across my soul. It was also in the church house that Bob was seen doing drugs in the bathroom! The Pastor sent an elder to confront Bob—another life-altering moment for him! The love of Christ pulling on his heart through the love he received from our church!

Sunday morning, June 9, 1996, things were literally at their worst. I couldn't take another moment of living the way we were. I sat with the choir behind our Pastor, and Bob was sitting with Joshua out in the crowd as Pastor Ray preached the morning's message. People around me probably thought I was taking notes on his sermon, but the truth was, I was planning the divorce. I had drawn a line down the middle of the paper, trying to decide how we would divide things. When I got to Joshua, I thought, "God, what am I going to do? Joshua needs his daddy, but not like this." The pain and thought of raising Joshua in a broken home shattered my heart.

God whispered across my soul again, "*Stay married!*"

"OK. FINE. I WILL STAY MARRIED, BUT YOU HAVE GOT TO TAKE OVER AND FIX THIS BECAUSE I CAN'T TAKE IT ANYMORE!" was my response. I am not proud of how I spoke to our awesome God, but this is just the plain truth. At this defining moment, I finally submitted my will to God.

> *For it is [not your strength, but it is] God who is effectively at work in you, both to will and to work [that is, strengthening, energizing, and creating in you the longing and the ability to fulfill your purpose] for His good pleasure.*
> **Philippians 2:13 AMP**

Friday morning, June 14, 1996, just five days later, Joshua (4 yrs. old at the time) and I found Bob face first on our living room floor. Drug paraphernalia was all around him; I thought he was dead from an overdose. It was at that point that Jesus literally took over! And I mean literally. A popular poem called *Footprints In The Sand* talks about our life being reflected by two sets of footprints walking along the shoreline, one being ours, the other belonging to Jesus. The poem continues to say that at times we may only see one set of prints, thinking that we were alone, but when there was one set of prints, those were the times that Jesus was carrying us. Well, on this day, Jesus was not carrying me. He literally took over, directing my every move and speaking my every word . . .

When Bob opened his eyes, he said the first thing he saw was Josh's face and thought, "I can't lose another family." He roused himself up and went into the family bathroom at the end of a long hallway in between two bedrooms, one being Joshua's room. Joshua was standing right outside the closed door. I sat on the edge of the tub while Bob sat on the toilet. I spoke these words, "Bob, I love you, and I will love you no matter what. But you have a choice to make. It's either me and Joshua or your drinking and drugging. I will not raise our son in this mess." I believe with all my heart that it was God speaking directly to Bob through me at that moment, the peace and love that was present with us was overwhelming.

I left the house and took Joshua to daycare. On the way back, I phoned ARC (Addiction Recovery Center), and they told me the same thing they had before when I had called for help. I was the wrong one making the call—Bob needed to make the call himself if he wanted help. As I drove up the long driveway to the house, desperate and crushed, I longed for Bob to make the call.

All for Jesus, Bob

He did! On June 14, 1996, we checked him into the Addiction Recovery Center at Tallahassee Community Hospital.

Sometime during that day, I must have called my sister for help and direction. She is a nurse practitioner and was working at the time with a doctor that helped patients with drug addictions. (The doctor she worked for was the one that treated Bob in the hospital.) Anyway, I had no sooner gotten home from settling Bob in the hospital when she walked in the door asking, "Are you ready to go?"

"What do you mean?" I asked.
"I'm here to help you pack," she said.
"What are you talking about?" I asked her. "I'm not going anywhere."
She said, "You're not leaving him?"
"No," I replied.
"What are you going to do?" she asked.
"I don't know, Therese. I really don't know anything right now except for one thing. I'm staying married."

All for Jesus, Bob

Chapter 3—Out Of The Pit

Trust in the Lord with all your heart, And lean not on your own understanding. In all your ways acknowledge Him, And He shall direct your paths.
Proverbs 3:5-6 NKJV

Bob was in the hospital Friday evening through Wednesday morning. We weren't able to visit until Sunday, which was Father's Day. His check-in on Friday was the last time I saw or spoke to him. On that Sunday, Joshua and I brought him his Bible, a WWJD bracelet, and a bookmark Joshua had made for him in pre-school. (He wore that bracelet until it fell off over ten years later!) As he read his Bible after we left that day, the Lord led him to Proverbs Chapter 3, verses 5 and 6 (see above) stood out to him. He was so touched by these words that he re-dedicated his life to the Lord.

His conversation with Jesus, the Living Word, went something like this:

"Bob, trust Me with all your heart, stop leaning on your own understanding, stop trying to figure things out on your own. In all your ways acknowledge Me, and I promise to direct your paths," Jesus said to him.

"Lord, I've tried it all. I've tried the fast cars, fast women, the money, the alcohol, the drugs, all this, none of it, none of it brought me what I wanted. So I give up and give myself to you. I'm going to give you the next year. I promise for the next year to get up every day, read Your Word, and do my best to do what it says. I will try it Your way Lord because my way landed me right here in this rehab facility. The best I could do brought me here on Father's Day, with my wife and four-year-old son visiting a strung-out alcoholic drug addict. If You will have me, take this shot-out mess of a life that I've created and do with it as You will." Bob replied. His surrender to Jesus came just one week after mine.

He also brought me up out of a horrible pit, Out of the miry clay, And set my feet upon a rock, And established my steps.
Psalm 40:2 NKJV

Sometimes God asks us to stay in the pit before He brings us out! When He asked me to stay married to Bob, He was asking me to stay in the pit.

Bob's recovery program was outpatient. After being released from the hospital, he followed the protocol they gave him to the T. He was given the 90/30 AA program,

All for Jesus, Bob

ninety meetings in thirty days. That meant that he was going to AA meetings three times a day for the next thirty days, and he didn't miss one! He also didn't miss a morning in prayer and the Word as he had committed to Jesus. It was a very rare occasion indeed if he was not up spending time with Jesus, as he would say, "before the rest of the world tries to crowd Him out." He continued the same 'treatment' plan for a long time—heeding the advice he had heard an AA leader give to another newcomer. When the newcomer asked the leader, "How many meetings do I have to attend to stay sober?" The leader's advice was, "Just start cutting back one a day until you are drunk again, and then you'll know."

He also attended church services every time there was one and soon became very involved in service at the church. His first job was picking up trash from the pews after each service had ended. I remember him telling me that it was a great honor to do that! He counted it a great privilege to be a servant in God's house, regardless of the task.

Things were going so well for Bob but not so much for me; I recall saying to him, "Things might be better for you, but they are still horrible for me!"

Bob was what we later dubbed "HJF"—happy, joyous, and free. He didn't just go to the AA meetings; he did the grueling hard work of the twelve steps and obeying the

Word of God. They changed his life! He found a new way of living! He was doing the next right thing, no matter the cost or how hard it was. On the other hand, I didn't trust the change I saw in him, and I was jealous of his joy.

My road to recovery was a little different. On the day I settled Bob into ARC, I sat in front of a counselor sobbing. Questioning aloud, "How did I get here? How did I end up with a strung-out drug addict for a husband? What am I going to do? What do I do now? What do I *do*?"

The counselor's response was gentle and to the point, "Educate yourself." He explained that Bob had a disease, and just like any other disease, I needed to learn about it and how to treat it. He suggested I read the AA Book, and at a minimum, he said to read the chapter titled "To The Wives." Additionally, he recommended that I attend all of the recovery center's family meetings.

I went to the family meetings expecting them to be focused on the addict, but much to my surprise, I learned more about myself! The meeting started where I thought it would, with the teacher describing all the signs and symptoms of an alcoholic/drug addict. But she quickly changed course, and I discovered that I was co-dependent and had just as many issues as an addict! As she explained the symptoms of a co-dependent, she was reading my mail, as they say! I was shocked at how the symptoms of both were strikingly similar. I'll be honest and blunt; I was as sick as Bob was! Having accepted this truth, I embarked on my own recovery journey.

Although I tried the Al-Anon meetings, they simply weren't for me. God had another route for me to take. I was fortunate to be working a position within a mortgage company as a Loan Officer. My schedule was flexible, so when I was invited to participate in a ladies' Bible study class, I agreed and started to attend.

There was an incredible and hilarious moment at the first class I went to. The teacher for the class was a beautiful blond hair blue-eyed woman. She looked and acted like an angel! The sweetest smile you will ever see caused her eyes to sparkle with joy. Anyway, she started that class with these words, "Today, ladies, we are going to talk about submitting to our husbands."

"What???" was the first thought in my mind. "NO way! She is insane! She obviously doesn't know anything about who I am married to! NO WAY I am going to submit to Bob!" As I was thinking these thoughts, I got up to leave, but my butt was glued to the chair! There was a presence in that room, keeping me seated and listening. Thank God! He kept me there that day and kept me coming back, and I'm very grateful to Him for that.

Both Bob and I were very involved in Bible study and attending church. Even though Bob was voted 'least likely to succeed' at ARC, his success was extraordinary because of his positive outlook and level of commitment. Despite these achievements, as I stated earlier, I didn't trust the changes I saw. I was still broken and hurting deeply. Every day I anticipated the other shoe to drop—asking myself, "Is this the day that he's going to drink again?" Or "Is today the day he won't come home for several days?"

> *"You can't go wrong doing right, so when you don't know what to do, just do the next right thing."*
> *–Pastor Bob*

Bob worked very hard to rebuild the trust that was broken between us. If he was going somewhere and was supposed to be home at five o'clock and saw that it would be a minute after five before making it to the house, he would call me and tell me he would be a minute or two late. He was tenacious about doing the next right thing and being a man of his word. He lived by the advice he often gave others, "You can't go wrong doing right, so when you don't know what to do, just do the next right thing."

On the other hand, I was still living in my anger, which imprisoned me. No doubt I was growing in my knowledge of the Lord, but I was not experiencing the same joy and freedom that Bob was, and as I stated before, it made me very angry. I felt he didn't deserve happiness after putting me through so much hell! His joy irked me so much that often I would just as soon spit in his face, smack him, or throw him out of the house, as look at him! Not proud moments of my past—but I'm being real!

> *Delight yourself also in the Lord, And He shall give you the desires of your heart.*
> **Psalm 37:4 NKJV**

I longed to have Bob's joy but didn't know how to obtain it. Despite all our turmoil, our family was blessed with the addition of our daughter, Jacquelyn Lee, in March 1997. Following my maternity leave, I returned to work as a loan officer with Wells Fargo. At the time, I was doing Beth Moore's Bible study called **A Heart Like His, Seeking the Heart of God Through a Study of David**, and reading Neil Anderson's book, **The Bondage Breaker**. My habit at the time was getting up at six o'clock in the morning to do Bible study before waking the children and starting our day for school, the sitter, and work.

> *And be kind to one another, tenderhearted, forgiving one another, even as God in Christ forgave you.*
> **Ephesians 4:32 NKJV**

One Monday morning, while in my quiet time with the Lord, we were having a conversation that went like this:

"I don't understand why Bob is so happy, joyous, and free. It seems that this would be the other way around, that I should be the one happy, joyous and free, and he should be miserable for all the problems he has caused our family and me. It doesn't seem right or fair."

"We can fix that, Laura," God spoke to me. "Here's your issue; you are a very angry, bitter, and resentful woman. You have ABR—Anger, Bitterness, Resentment."

As God held up that mirror, I clearly saw and admitted that He was right. I had ABR! "But what does that have to do with me being HJF like Bob?" I asked.

Confronted with my issue and agreeing with Him, He graciously continues, "If you'd like to get rid of your ABR and be like Bob, you need to forgive him."

"What?? No way! I'm not forgiving him! You don't know what he has done to me! That would be totally unfair and not right!" I slammed my Bible closed and my workbook and went on with my day.

Tuesday morning, I returned to my desk for quiet time at six o'clock. I had been having an incredible time in Bible studies discovering new treasures. Moving forward and expecting to find more of these treasures, I began the next day's work in the workbook. But God had a different plan. We were in the same place, Ephesians 4:32. Not

All for Jesus, Bob

letting me move forward, God re-stated, "If you want what Bob has, you need to forgive him."

"No!" I emphatically replied. "This is ridiculous! This doesn't even make any sense! He doesn't deserve my forgiveness! All the hurt he has caused our family, that he has caused me—no way I can forgive him. I don't think You understand." Closing my Bible and workbook firmly, I left again and went on with my day.

Wednesday morning. I came back for quiet time again, certain that we were moving forward and that today I would discover new treasures in the Word of God. But, again, as I said, God had a different plan, and He wasn't changing His mind! As I try to begin the next day's work in the workbook, He tells me again, "Laura, if you want what Bob has, you need to forgive him."

"No!!" I start my childish rant again. "Bob does not deserve my forgiveness! You don't know the hurt and pain he has caused me! This is not fair! HE DOES NOT DESERVE to be forgiven!"

God interrupted my rant and gently replied, "Laura, neither did you deserve my forgiveness."

I fell to my knees at these words, my face in my hands and my head face-first on the chair. Weeping, I respond, "Lord, I am so sorry . . . how right you are! I didn't deserve

Your forgiveness. Thank You. I will forgive Bob, but I have a problem; I don't know how. Please show me how."

I got up from that prayer time and went on with my day. On Wednesdays, we had staff meetings at ten o'clock in the morning. That very day the receptionist interrupted our meeting and stated that there was someone upfront insisting on seeing me. "Did you tell them I was in this meeting?" I asked.

"Yes," she replied. "They insist that they must see you right now."

Excusing myself from the meeting, I went up front. The person there handed me three sheets of paper, stapled in the upper left-hand corner, and folded in half. "God told me that I needed to bring this to you right now." They said as they handed it to me and then turned and left. I turned and headed back to the meeting. As I walked there, I opened the paper and was stunned at the title, "How To Forgive!"

Unbelievable! God had just answered my prayer and sent me step-by-step instructions on how to forgive Bob! No one will ever convince me that God is not real and that He does not hear our cries! No one, and I mean no one else, heard our conversation that morning! Each day's conversation was in my heart with Him, not out loud, and it was just between the two of us![1]

The Farmer & The Donkey

One day a farmer's donkey fell down into a well. The animal cried piteously for hours as the farmer tried to figure out a way to get him out. Finally, he decided it was probably impossible and the animal was old and the well was dry

---

[1] If you'd like a copy of this paper that was handed to me, you may e-mail me and I will gladly share it! Or you can obtain a copy of Neil Anderson's book **The Bondage Breaker**, you will find it under Step 3 of the 7 Steps to Freedom in Christ found in the appendix of his book.

anyway, so it just wasn't worth it to try and retrieve the donkey. So the farmer asked his neighbors to come over and help him cover up the well. They all grabbed shovels and began to shovel dirt into the well.

At first, when the donkey realized what was happening he cried horribly. Then, to everyone's amazement, he quieted down and let out some happy brays. A few shovel loads later, the farmer looked down the well to see what was happening and was astonished at what he saw. With every shovel of dirt that hit his back, the donkey was shaking it off and taking a step up.

As the farmer's neighbors continued to shovel dirt on top of the animal, he continued to shake it off and take a step up. Pretty soon, to everyone's amazement, the donkey stepped up over the edge of the well and trotted off!

The way to get out of the deepest well is by never giving up but by shaking yourself off and taking a step up. What happens to you isn't nearly as important as how you react to it.

Author Unknown

All for Jesus, Bob

I could hardly wait to get alone with God again and follow His instructions! I did, and may I say, my life has never been the same! To God be the glory, I unloaded the weight of my sin of unforgiveness and found His joy! I felt as if the weight of the world had been lifted off of my shoulders! The Lord had given me my heart's desire! I was now HJF! As you can imagine, this made an incredible difference in our marriage! I was a new woman! Bob no longer had to find the corner of the roof to escape my contentiousness! Forgiveness—what a priceless gift!

Bible study, AA meetings, and church were integral parts of our recovery. I didn't think I was working the Twelve Steps, but I was! God led me through them via the Bible studies I was participating in. We have since learned that the AA steps work so well because they are straight out of the Bible!

God's ways always work! They may seem foreign to us and be just the opposite of what we think is right, but truly, His way is the best way to find our way to being HJF, happy, joyous, and free!

All for Jesus, Bob

My brethren, count it all joy when you fall into various trials, knowing that the testing of your faith produces patience. But let patience have its perfect work, that you may be perfect and complete, lacking nothing.
James 1:2-4 NKJV

Watching Bob enjoy his newfound freedom in Christ and not having it myself made me feel that God had left me in the pit. What felt like God heaving piles of dirt on my head was nothing of the sort! It was Him helping me make my way out! It is hard to see it when the dirt hits the top of your head and flies in your face, but the trials are for our good!

I liken each step of our recovery, staying married, going to meetings, Bible study, admitting our wrongs, church services, seeking forgiveness from those we've wronged, and choosing forgiveness, to a shovel of dirt thrown on our heads. To God be the glory! We shook off the dirt, patted it down, and made steps! We then walked up the steps and got out of the pit!

Chapter 4—Serving & Being Rebuilt

And so now I'll start over with you and build you up again, dear virgin Israel. You'll resume your singing, grabbing tambourines and joining the dance.
Jeremiah 31:4 MSG

I am considered to be a Type A personality. Driven, hardworking, and determined to succeed. Type A people are doers! I always feel a need to be *doing* something. Which is why the day I settled Bob in at ARC, I asked the counselor, "What am I going to do?" I recall with a smile in my heart my mom saying to me when I was a child, "Go and find *something* to do, even if it's wrong!" There was not much sitting around and doing nothing in my childhood home!

This information about me should explain our being very active in our local church. We didn't just attend the services on Sunday morning and evening and Wednesday evening—we served. We *did* stuff. Bob started cleaning up the pews after the services, and I joined the choir and served in the nursery. He went to AA meetings; I went to Bible study. Bob was up every morning before the rest of the house praying and in the Word. When the church offered a Bible study called **Experiencing God**, Bob went.

His hunger for the Word increased, and a desire for fellowship with other Christian men caused him to join a small men's group that met once per week at a local restaurant to study the Word and pray. He also started working with me in the nursery!

We took our places of service and Bible studies very seriously. When Bob and I worked in the 1-2-year-old nursery together, we didn't just watch the children. We sat on the floor with them and taught them. Holding our Bible, we would teach them that it was a Bible and that the Bible was God's Word. By the time they graduated up to the 2-3-year-olds, they had it down pat! They could hold a Bible and say, "This is a Bible. The Bible is God's Word." We would also share simple stories with them from the Bible, planting the seed of His Word in their precious hearts, praying it would take root and grow.

Your promises are the source of my bubbling joy; the revelation of your word thrills me like one who has discovered hidden treasure.
Psalm 119:162 TPT

In our Bible studies, we *did* the homework! (I, unfortunately, see many Bible study books coming into our ministry for donation where the participant did the first day or first few days and never finished. What a tragedy! They missed out on many treasures by not finishing!) The joy truly bubbled up in us as we discovered hidden treasures of truth regarding our salvation and our behaviors. The Word of God is sharper than any two-edged sword; it pierces us to our core and reveals the thoughts and intents of our hearts. The Word showed us where we were wrong and how to make it right!

After some time, Bob and I started doing the same Bible studies, which was another game-changer for us! The first class we did together was called, **A Biblical Portrait of Marriage**. We both faced some serious truths about how far off our marriage was from being what the Bible said it should be. God had so much more for us! Our marriage was transformed as we both did the hard work of studying, communicating, and submitting to God. We discovered a level of connection, love, and loyalty to God and each other that carried us for the rest of our married life. One of the most interesting and best things that happened to us as we did these different studies together was that our conversation changed.

We were no longer in the blame game, arguing or fighting. We were discussing the treasures we had found in the Word of God. We found ourselves praying together, yes together, as a couple on our knees, voicing out loud our concerns and desires before the throne of God. Talk about connecting—when you are before the Truth in truth, the intimacy level created is off the chain. Moreover, we began to seek each other out, asking questions about how each of us behaved and treated each other in an effort to understand each other and make the necessary changes to become the best husband and wife possible. We had a common goal: glorify God and maintain the newfound peace and joy in our lives and home.

> *And do not be conformed to this world, but be transformed by the renewing of your mind, that you may prove what is that good and acceptable and perfect will of God.*
> **Romans 12:2 NKJV**

Being involved in these activities offered us good, positive things to do and focus on. We truly felt and experienced the love of the Lord. We knew we were accepted and felt the warmth of the love of God and his people. Bob had someone tell him once that he had been brainwashed because he was all about Jesus and so active in the church—to which he replied, "Yep! My brain needed washing!"

"My brain needed washing!" –Pastor Bob

The Bible studies and singing involved a lot of memory work! Songs sung by the ladies' ensemble I was privileged to be part of were performed from memory. The Christmas cantata required doing all the songs from memory as well, so I listened to the music every chance I

All for Jesus, Bob

could to work on memorizing it all. Some of the Bible studies I participated in required memorizing Scriptures, too, so as I did these things—I was being transformed. And likewise, Bob, except for the singing!

The very first time the ladies' ensemble was scheduled to sing for the church happened to land on Bob's one-year clean and sober anniversary. We were scheduled for the Sunday evening service; unbeknownst to me, Bob had shared that it was his anniversary with our Pastor, Pastor Ray, after the morning's service. As the evening service started, I sat with the ladies' group two sections away from Bob and Josh, where we normally sat together. I was a nervous wreck! I didn't think I belonged with these incredibly talented and perfectly Christian ladies, let alone a good enough singer to be on stage in front of a large crowd!

Before we were called up to sing, Pastor Ray spoke to Bob from the pulpit, "Bob, you shared some good news with me this morning. Is it ok if I share it with the church?" To which Bob replied, "Of course! Go for it, Pastor!" As Pastor Ray shared that Bob was celebrating one year clean and sober and a few other of our sordid details, I thought I would die of embarrassment! No one (that I knew of) knew of my plight at home! Surely now that these ladies knew what my home life was like, they'd likely kick me out of the group, and maybe the choir director and nursery director would think I'd be better serving elsewhere! Despite my fear and humiliation, I went on stage with the group to sing (and there were surely at least two hundred people there), and the song's title was, **I Am A Walking Talking Testimony Of What The Lord Can Do!**

God has an amazing sense of timing! After singing, we sat with our respective families for the remainder of the service. After it was over, I avoided everyone and went straight home. I spent the rest of my evening wrestling with whether or not I would go to the scheduled lunch the ladies' ensemble had the next day. Fearful, but knowing I'd have to face the music sometime (no pun intended), I went to the lunch. No one spoke about what Pastor Ray had disclosed the night before! When I could no longer bear it, I asked, "Well, do you ladies want me to leave the group?"

"What? Why?" they asked. "Because of what Pastor Ray disclosed about our family last night," I responded.

"No!" they all emphatically told me. "We love you, Laura. We are just sorry you didn't feel comfortable enough to share your burden with us so we could pray with you and help you through your tough time." See! What love! What acceptance! What warmth! That group was a blessing—totally part of God's plan and timing to transform my heart and life. Grateful does not even begin to explain what I feel towards God and all those ladies I was privileged to serve beside for many years!

Brothers and sisters, if someone is caught in a sin, you who live by the Spirit should restore that person gently. But watch yourselves, or you also may be tempted.
Galatians 6:1 NIV

When Bob reached the twelfth step of the AA program, which says, "Having had a spiritual awakening as the result of these Steps, we tried to carry this message to alcoholics, and to practice these principles in all our affairs."[2] He treated that like every other step, took it very seriously, and started living it.

He began serving at local rescue missions while continuing his service at the church. He traveled to a

---

[2] https://www.aa.org/the-twelve-steps

men's residential recovery program early Sunday mornings to pick guys up and bring them to church. He would bring friends and strangers to stay at our home to help them get sober. They would stay with us until he could find a place to get them help. In one case, he allowed someone to stay with us for several months until he got on his own two feet again. I remember the first man he brought home . . . his name was Ron. Ron was an ophthalmologist. When we drove to work one day, we saw him in the corner of the parking lot . . . obviously homeless. He had all of his worldly belongings with him.

As soon as we saw him, I knew Bob would go and speak to him, offering him help. We parked the car, Bob went and talked to him, and I went into the office and called a prayer partner, and we prayed for them. Bob brought him home that day, washed his clothes for him, and found him a place that he could go to within a couple of days. I haven't spoken to Ron in a long time, but he was doing great the last time I did! He had gotten back on his feet, was working again, and living right! To God be the glory!

> *A man's heart plans his way,*
> *But the LORD directs his steps.*
> **Proverbs 16:9 NKJV**

As we continued serving, God directed Bob to serve in Awana and called me to "teach and pray."

All for Jesus, Bob

"Awana is a world-wide nonprofit ministry focused on providing Bible-based evangelism and discipleship solutions for ages 2-18. As the global leader in child and youth discipleship, Awana gives children the opportunity to know, love and serve Jesus, no matter their background."[3] As Bob served as a leader for the children in this program, God gave him a vision that caused him to quit smoking and chewing tobacco. (He was a 3-pack-a-day smoker and chewed on top of that!) He was also blessed to have a couple of mentors that took him under his wing during this same time.

Pastor Horne used to take him out on church visitation; he would tell him, "Bob, you smell awful, but let's go anyway!" He was captivated as he watched Pastor Horne share the Gospel with each family they visited. Doing these things gave Bob a sense of purpose and revealed his true heart's desire. He would spend the rest of his life sharing the Gospel however the Lord led him to!

One Sunday morning, as I was getting ready to go to church, God spoke to my heart, "I want you to teach and pray. Go tell Bob and tell Jan Ray." I obeyed immediately and went and told Bob what the Lord had spoken to me and when I walked into church that morning, the first person I ran into was Jan Ray, and I told her. I quickly

---

[3] https://www.awana.org/about/

began teaching a ladies' Sunday School class—again finding myself where I felt I did not belong! Who was I to teach these ladies? They surely were far better Christians and more knowledgeable about the Bible than I was! Sharing my fears and concerns with the Lord in prayer, He responds with the following:

> *Then the word of the Lord came to me, saying:*
> *"Before I formed you in the womb I knew you;*
> *Before you were born I sanctified you; I ordained*
> *you a prophet to the nations."*
> *Then said I: "Ah, Lord God! Behold,*
> *I cannot speak, for I am a youth."*
> *But the Lord said to me: "Do not say, 'I am a youth,'*
> *For you shall go to all to whom I send you,*
> *And whatever I command you, you shall speak.*
> *Do not be afraid of their faces,*
> *For I am with you to deliver you," says the Lord.*
> *⁹ Then the Lord put forth His hand and touched my*
> *mouth, and the Lord said to me:*
> *"Behold, I have put My words in your mouth.*
> *¹⁰ See, I have this day set you over the nations*
> *and over the kingdoms,*
> *To root out and to pull down, To destroy and to*
> *throw down, To build and to plant."*
> **Jeremiah 1:4-10 NKJV**

I have counted on Him to keep His promise to me ever since—and He has!

All for Jesus, Bob

One Sunday evening, Pastor Ray brought the FAITH Evangelism to our church. As we were nearing the end of the service, I knew that Pastor Ray would be giving an altar call, asking those interested in learning how to share the Gospel to come forward. I knew Bob would respond. I also knew that I was to participate by starting a prayer group in our home to pray for all the teams going out and sharing the Gospel and for all the people hearing it. Bob was out of his seat and at the altar before Pastor Ray finished the first sentence of his invitation.

Bob and I both did several of what they call FAITH semesters. During this time, we developed some deep friendships with those that were like-hearted. We started a Bible study with them in our home, and it was during this Bible study ChristTown Ministries Inc. was birthed. As I write these words, it is hard to believe that that was twenty years ago!

> *Better a day in Your courts than a thousand anywhere else. I would rather be at the door of the house of my God than to live in the tents of wicked people.*
> **Psalm 84:10 HCSB**

Truly as the Psalmist says, better is one day in His house than a thousand elsewhere! The molding and shaping God does in and through us as we choose to come to Him just as we are and begin serving any way we can is nothing short of a miracle! Bob and I were flawed people searching for a better way of life, and we found it while serving and being rebuilt.

Chapter 5—Changing Locks

For you see your calling, brethren, that not many wise according to the flesh, not many mighty, not many noble, are called.
1 Corinthians 1:26 NKJV

Bob was sitting in one of our regular Sunday morning services when he heard the Holy Spirit ask him to commit to being a full-time servant. He responded to this call with a yes and put action to his answer by moving over in his seat on the pew and then telling me about it that day when we were done with Sunday lunch. I recall asking him, "What will you be doing?"

"I don't know," was his response. "But God does, and I will wait for him to show me." It would not be the only time I heard these words from him!

The answer to my question regarding what he would be doing came clearly during the group Bible study I spoke about in the last chapter. A gentleman named Glenn was in that Bible study, and both he and Bob had hearts for the down and out. Glenn, at that time, was the director of a ministry called The Haven of Rest. The Haven was a residential home in downtown Tallahassee that ministered to homeless men. Bob, as I previously stated, was very involved in this ministry.

During this time, Bob and I worked together in a mortgage business that we ran from an office on our homestead property. One day as I was sorting through a pile of faxes, I was about to throw away one advertising some commercial property in Quincy, FL. At the time, I had no idea why, but I kept it in my hand instead of putting it in the trash and walked over and placed it on Bob's desk. When Bob saw it, he was moved to go and check it out. He called Glenn, and they went on a scouting trip to Quincy to see the property. When they came back—I could feel the glory of God several hundred feet before they pulled in by the office to park! They were glowing! They shared with me how God had met them on the property, and they were one thousand percent sure that we would begin our ministry in that location. We were going to rescue the perishing and care for the dying! ChristTown would begin in Quincy, Florida!

When praying together about how we would finance this new venture, Bob heard the Lord tell him, "you are kneeling on it." He knew then that he would have to sell the homestead property; it was a property given to him and his sister by their father. This meant calling Martha Ann, his sister, and telling her he was ready to sell. We were living in the house on that property at the time.

All for Jesus, Bob

He called Martha Ann right away and told her what God had called him to do and asked her if she would be willing to sell. Her response was a miracle! Not only did she say she would sell, but she added, "I'm going with you!" To understand what a miracle this was, we sold that property for over a million dollars! To have two siblings agree to take that kind of money and give it all to the Lord! Wow! I was stunned, and to this day, I stand in awe of how God works in the hearts of His people. The unity and peace between those two and the lack of arguing about their inheritance still amazes me!

Me? Well, the questions started rolling in! We were selling the place where our family lived and giving it all to start the ministry; where would we live? Where would the children go to school? Where would Josh play ball? How would we afford anything? I asked Bob each of these questions—and his reply? "I don't know, Laura, but God does. We will wait and see how He works it out." Uggghh! The frustration I felt at his fierce solid faith! How could he be so calm? It was going to be a world-shaking experience, and he appeared to not have a care in the world about it all!

God is our refuge and strength, A very present help in trouble. Therefore we will not fear, Even though the earth be removed, And though the mountains be carried into the midst of the sea; Though its waters roar and be troubled, Though the mountains shake with its swelling. Selah
Psalm 46:1-3 NKJV

Here we go again! He was at total peace; I was a wreck until . . . the morning God woke me up at 4 am. I headed towards my desk to start reading the Bible when I sensed He wanted me on my knees beside the bed praying. As I knelt, in my audacity, I asked Him what He needed me to pray about . . . *nothing, Laura . . .*, and in the next few moments, He answered all the 'what about' questions I had! He made it clear that He had Bob, and it was my job to follow and support him. This encounter with our awesome God filled me to the brim with peace! He had calmed the storm of my heart. The raging river of questions no longer existed, God was with us, and that was enough.

for it is God who works in you both to will and to do for His good pleasure.
Philippians 2:13 NKJV

I crawled back into the bed and slept soundly. When I awoke, I went straight to Bob, shared my experience with him, and said, "No more questions. God is with you, and

He is with us! I will follow you and do whatever I can to help." God, the Author and Finisher of our faith, had filled us both with what we needed for the journey.

So, Raymond Diehl Road goes up for sale! We took out a line of credit on the house to secure the property in Quincy and help pay the bills on it until Raymond Diehl sold. I continued running the mortgage business to pay the bills at home. The property in Quincy was three separate pieces. It had a 23-unit motel, a 22,000-square-foot warehouse, and a twelve-room boarding house across the main highway. The plan was to house women and children or families in the hotel rooms and single men in the boarding house. The warehouse would become a thrift store to help fund the ministry. The hotel was called The Creation One Inn; I found that to be interesting, as God is our Creator!

The moment the property in Quincy was secured, it took no time to fill up. It was Thursday evening, August 1, 2002, when Bob got a call from Glenn, "I have our first ChristTown residents; I have a couple in need of a place to stay." Without hesitation, Bob left to meet Glenn in Quincy at the hotel to welcome and settle in the first people he was honored and privileged to rescue from perishing. This couple stayed with us for quite some time, helping manage the day-to-day activities.

All for Jesus, Bob

The Lord has appeared of old to me, saying:
"Yes, I have loved you with an everlasting love;
Therefore with lovingkindness I have drawn you.
Jeremiah 31:3 NKJV

Within what seemed like days, the facility was completely full! We were housing some sixty-plus women and children and twenty-four men! Wondering how this happened? Me too! In His great mercy and mysterious ways, God led them to us.

I remember Bob putting out a little yard sign in front of the conference center; this drew some people to us. Others happened in extraordinary ways, like the time when I answered the phone, "ChristTown Ministries, may I help you?"

"Who is this?" the caller asked.
"ChristTown Ministries."
"This isn't The Creation One Inn?"
"No," I responded, "We are a new ministry that helps people in need; there hasn't been enough time to change it in the phone book."
"You, you, help people..." said the man on the other end of the phone.
"Yes, do you need help?"
"Yes!"

All for Jesus, Bob

I turned the call over to Bob, and the gentleman came to ChristTown to get help to get out of his addictive lifestyle! The man had been sitting in a hotel room in Tallahassee, over thirty miles away, crying for help. He was desperate. He said he kept hearing in his mind, *call The Creation One Inn in Quincy, FL,* over and over until he finally did and got me on the other end of the phone! Miracles!!! Our God is still in the miracle business! He hears our cries and is close to the broken-hearted. He wants to help us up, and out of the pits we find ourselves in!

> ***But God hath chosen the foolish things of the world to confound the wise; and God hath chosen the weak things of the world to confound the things which are mighty.***
> **1 Corinthians 1:27 KJV**

When we first started, we did not know what we were doing! We just knew we were sent to love and help people! We started by meeting their physical needs, sharing the love of Christ and the Gospel, and carrying them to church. Bob shared his experience, strength, and hope with them, assuring them that if God could deliver him from being an addict, He could help them too!

We held church services Wednesday and Sunday evenings in the dining room area of the hotel until the local Catholic church donated their old wooden pews to us. We set them up in the front of the conference center, making a chapel for the ministry. Sunday mornings, we (our family and all the ChristTown residents) attended services at different churches in the area after we held a Sunday School service in the chapel. We had been ministering for over a year when Bob had an unction to *stay home* and start doing Sunday morning church services in our chapel.

I held a Sunday school class for the children, and Bob did the adults. It was amazing to see the difference in the lives of those children with a little attention and some stability! I would make a point to ask how their week was at school, how their grades were doing, and see if they needed any extra help. Bob would make a point each day to greet them as they came in from school, asking how their day was.

Knowing that they would have food, a safe place to sleep, and someone asking about their day created an environment where they could thrive. Their improvement was so noticeable that one of the school's officials even commented on it! These children were experiencing the peace and love of Jesus. It had a powerful impact on their lives and it was reflected in their grades and behavior at school.

We worked hard to minister the same to the adults! We were learning the hard way what worked and what didn't

All for Jesus, Bob

for helping the addict. We discovered quickly that money and a phone were two things we needed to keep away from the addict to increase their chances of success. I recall as I write that as Bob was getting clean and sober, he had no money. When he came to work with me in the mortgage business, he got twenty dollars a week and a bag of mints! With which he was thrilled! My income covered all of his other needs, including food, clothes, and the bills.

Too often, Bob found himself intervening between our resident and the drug dealer. Our initial thought was that if we could get them working and focused in the right direction, they'd be doing good . . . but nope! The paycheck would come, and they would beat feet to the drug dealer. We found ourselves doing crazy things like following them to crack houses or the drug deal meeting to try and stop them from going down that path. I remember one woman in particular that had just captured my heart. She was one of the sweetest people you would ever meet. She had a beautiful smile—one that just melted your heart. One day as I saw the crack demon look come across her face, I tried to minister to her anger and desire to get high, but I lost. She took off, and I knew where she was headed, so I followed her!

Pulling right up the driveway of the crack house, about 15-20 people standing around, I asked for her . . . they looked into the front door of the house, which stood open. I walked up to the door hollering for her and they told me she had run out the back! Heartbroken, I walked back to my truck and went back to the ministry property. That was the only time I did that. The Lord showed me the danger I had placed myself in and that I was regressing into my co-dependent behaviors. As much as I wanted to, I could not make anyone do anything. We were learning to love the ones in front of us; if someone really wanted to change, they would just as we had. Our precious Jesus was offering them the same freedom He had given us.

> *And my God shall supply all your need according to His riches in glory by Christ Jesus.*
> **Philippians 4:19 NKJV**

Shortly, it became clear that I needed to quit doing mortgages and go full-time with Bob in the ministry. Between the ministering we were doing and the administrative work that needed to be done, there was not enough time to run both! As the Holy Spirit moved upon my heart to quit doing mortgages, I would like to say that I was full of faith by this time and just did it, but I didn't. I began asking questions, again, like, how would we pay our bills? ChristTown was not generating the first dime of income, just the opposite! We were pouring everything we had into it!

All for Jesus, Bob

The property on Raymond Diehl Rd. had not sold yet, and we were racking up the balance on our credit line! In the world, I saw no way that we could make it . . . but Bob, as always, saw through the eyes of faith! He told me on more than one occasion that he was willing to take our family to bankruptcy doing what God had told him to do. He was that sure. He was sure God would make a way for us; after all, He promised to supply *all* of our needs! So, I took the plunge, submitted again to the Holy Spirit, quit the mortgage business, and went full-time with ChristTown. Not knowing when, if, or how our next bill would be paid—despite my fears, I chose to place my trust in Jesus.

> *A man's heart plans his way,*
> *But the LORD directs his steps.*
> **Proverbs 16:9 NKJV**

During this same first year of starting up ChristTown, we were working on getting approval from the city commission. We worked hard to gather all the information and forms required to obtain approval to run the ministry at that location. We went to our first city commission meeting fully armed with all the paperwork and many people who supported us being there.

The commission seemed to agree, but they gave us a couple of additional things to do before they would approve our application and placed us on the schedule for the next meeting. The next month when we went back—it was just Bob, Martha Ann, and me. We were there to get our stamp of approval, but just the opposite happened! To our surprise, we watched the tide turn right before our eyes as all the 'yes's' turned into 'no's' when they took the vote. We were denied permission to operate our ministry in our location. We walked out of that meeting stunned and numb. What had just happened?

NIMyB. Not In My Back Yard, that's what happened. They all thought it was a great idea and a much-needed ministry, but not there. We received a "Cease and Desist" order a few days later. I'll never forget the day after we received that order. Bob and I prayed together at our bedside, seeking God's direction, approval, and encouragement. Grasping to find some understanding—as we were getting up from our knees, I asked Bob what he was going to do, "those are God's young'uns, Laura; I'm just His conduit. He will take care of them. I am not sure what's going to happen, but God does, and I will wait on Him. While we were praying, He showed me the next right thing to do. He showed some locks on doors that needed to be changed. I'm going to ChristTown and changing locks."

Chapter 6—Ministry of Reconciliation

A person may have many ideas concerning God's plan for his life, but only the designs of his purpose will succeed in the end.
Proverbs 19:21 TPT

Man may not have wanted ChristTown Ministries in Gadsden County, Florida, but God did. He apparently didn't want us in the location *we* thought He did! Things began to move pretty quickly after we got the "Cease and Desist" order. The order gave us thirty days to stop doing what we were doing. We had made our offer to purchase the Quincy property contingent upon the city and county permitting us to operate there. The commission's decline voided our contract.

The following is reprinted from our December 2003 newsletter, written by Bob:

"I must say I was surprised, to say the least, when the city commissioners of Quincy denied us the right to stay located at 412 S. Cooper St. (women's dorm & main office). I really felt the community was behind us, as residents, law enforcement, etc., were there to express their support. But evidently, God had a different plan.

We were voted down 3-2. I was unshaken by the decision knowing full well Who is in control of all, commissioners included. I have said many times, "I don't know what the future holds, but I do know Who holds the future!" I also know that He has thoughts of good for us and not of evil, and that all things work together for good to those who love the Lord and are called according to His purpose—these, my friends, are promises I run to every time the old wicked one tries to run a thread of doubt into my life.

I do know that I love the Lord with all my heart, I do know He has called me out for His work, and I do know He promises to direct my paths. If I seek His will and not mine, walk in obedience, and not allow myself to become still, hardened, and no longer pliable to the moving of His Holy Spirit, I am flooded with that precious peace that passes ALL UNDERSTANDING!

When I received a letter on November 4th stating that I had 30 days to get the women and children moved, I went directly to my Father for an answer, then waited…

I made an offer to Mr. Clary on the other two properties I was leasing (men's dorm and Chapel/warehouse future thrift store). He rejected it and asked for almost twice the amount I offered! Once again, I ran to "Daddy" for council. As always, He is faithful to lead us. By this time, we have three weeks to leave, and now I am faced with moving the women and children, the men, the church, plus tons of donations he has blessed us with and that are packed into the 22,000-square-foot warehouse. We know now that we are looking at a seriously GOD-SIZED task! But still, there was peace and no sign of panic among the people . . .

When He began to move, He moved us quickly!

I stopped by a dear Christian brother's shop to check on one of our residents who was employed there. During our conversation, he mentioned that his wife (who is a realtor) was putting in bids for a 5-bedroom home that was in foreclosure. We called his wife, I rode out and looked it over, prayed, put in a bid, got financing lined up, and we got it!

Next, as one of our residents was doing some painting and clean up for a local homeowner, she told him she was interested in renting or selling it. Another 5-6 bedroom home! I met with her, and we quickly reached a lease/option agreement.

Now, that still leaves us the 22,000 square feet of donations and Sanctuary without a home! There was one particular building I was drawn to, but the month before all this, I had called the realtor and inquired about leasing a portion of it. He said it was under contract, so there was no need to pursue it. Here I am again, Lord; I need you to show me what do I do?? He laid it on my heart to write up an offer on this building. I did just as he directed and sent it to the realtor. A day or so later, I got a call; it now seems we can make a deal with a few changes!

After solidifying the lease/option, I met with the owner to gain access to the property, and he began to want to change several things on the contract; this was making me uncomfortable. I called my bride and asked her to start praying that this confusion would be cleared and dismissed. Later that afternoon, we met again, and he decided to take the contract exactly as the Lord had directed me to write it! Now we can start moving! But there is only about a week left to get more than you can imagine moved. Our residents came together in such unity it was incredible; by Saturday afternoon, November 29th, we were moved with the exception of the Sanctuary, pews, piano, etc.

For our last Sunday morning service at this location, we were blessed to have one of my very dearest brothers in Christ scheduled to speak, Jim Horne, a missionary from Africa, brought us an incredible message from the Lord, and we were thrilled and honored by his presence and that of his dear wife, Susie. After the morning worship service, we began to disassemble the Sanctuary with the undying devotion of our residents, and before dark, we were relocated into our new home! 12,000 square feet of store and Sanctuary, and over 22,000 square feet of storage and shop space on over 6 acres of land, the place is absolutely HUGE! Yes, my dear brothers and sisters, our God is an awesome God!

We had the men, women & children, store, and the church relocated with four days to spare on the city's notice to leave! I'm still just standing back with my jaw dropped at how much happened in such a short time! I tell you honestly, this "walking by faith" is far from boring!

Thank You, Jesus!! Thank You!! We owe You our all!!!"

The headline for the newsletter was **Thanksgiving Miracle Move!** One year later, while we were waiting for God to provide His peace for us concerning buying the home for the women, He gave us a beautiful three-bedroom, two-bath home out in the country with an acre of planted blueberries! Again, I will say, our God is still in the miracle doing business!

> *And do not be conformed to this world, but be transformed by the renewing of your mind, that you may prove what is that good and acceptable and perfect will of God.*
> **Romans 12:2 NKJV**

By this time, the two years of on-the-job training by Jesus taught us a better way to help those that wanted it. The primary lesson we learned was that we could not help anyone who did not want help! I now had a much better understanding of why the Addiction Recovery Center told me I was the wrong one making the call. To set apart those that wanted help and those that didn't, the Lord gave us a set of rules that everyone would have to follow. We had our first exodus of residents as soon as we implemented these rules. Unfortunately, many there didn't want to change and refused to agree to abide by the new set of rules, so they left. This change significantly decreased the number of people we needed to move, and those who stayed fit nicely into the new homes God had provided.

As a result of the reduction in residents we were helping, the program became more of a program! We became more structured in our approach to helping each resident, and the Lord provided us with detailed program agreements for each resident to sign. The residents committed to giving the Lord one year, just as Bob had done when he first got clean and sober. Additionally, the resident agrees to all the requirements for them to receive a graduation certificate. For example, volunteer work in the thrift store and community and behavior standards. The main portions of this agreement remain standing today! Understanding that the only way they can be transformed is by renewing their minds, we added a required curriculum of classes, Scripture memorization, and book reports that each resident had to complete to graduate or get a certificate of completion from our ministry.[4]

> *Set your gaze on the path before you.*
> *With fixed purpose,*
> *looking straight ahead, ignore life's distractions.*
> *Watch where you're going! Stick to the path of truth,*
> *and the road will be safe and smooth before you.*
> *Don't allow yourself to be sidetracked for even a*
> *moment or take the detour that leads to darkness.*
> **Proverbs 4:25-27 TPT**

Another major change came somewhere around 2008. Even though the men and women lived in homes at opposite ends of town, rehab romances flourished. One look at each other across the pews or as they crossed paths during the day working at the thrift store was all it took for some to pair up and run off together! When praying about what to do, we were led to discontinue the ladies' portion of our program and house only men. Interestingly, this was what Bob was originally called to do, and Glenn and his wife were the ones that had a heart for the women. Glenn and Beth, by this time, had already started a mission in Tallahassee, which included a home for women. After making this change, the success rate of the men increased dramatically.

---

[4] The complete Phase 1 Program Agreement can be found on our website: www.christtown.org

Therefore, if anyone is in Christ, he is a new creation; old things have passed away; behold, all things have become new. Now all things are of God, who has reconciled us to Himself through Jesus Christ, and has given us the ministry of reconciliation,
2 Corinthians 5:17-18 NKJV

Throughout the years, the trials and tribulations, struggles, victories, and defeats, ChristTown Ministries Inc. has emerged as a church whose main focus is a men's residential drug and alcohol addiction recovery program. Our program is patterned after the program that Bob and I worked on as we recovered. Bob gave the Lord a year, so this is why we require the men to stay with us for a minimum of one year.

If you think about it, the first year is typically the hardest whenever there is the death of something. The first Christmas without someone, the first birthday, when you go fishing, or out to dinner. Stepping away from drugs and alcohol is a very similar process!

All for Jesus, Bob

The residents go through the first birthday without partying, the first Christmas, and the first time they fish or go home Friday evening after work for the weekend without using. During this first year, they are inundated with the Word of God, being brain-washed, some would say—but the truth is, the Word is renewing their minds and transforming them! (Romans 12:2) Doing volunteer work as part of the program, they are also learning how to be an excellent employee and deal with life issues according to the Word of God as they arise daily.

When the men enter our program, they are immediately changed from takers to givers! The work they do at the store provides help to the local community and, of course, aids in paying the bills in the home they live in!

When the men sign the program agreement, they commit to God to abide by the rules and understand that we are a faith-based program. The main requirement for them to gain entry into the program is the desire to want to change. They agree to no contact with the outside world for the first 60 days. After that, they are allowed to receive and write letters; after 90 days, they are allowed one phone call per week for 15 minutes.

For continued success, it is important to learn how to cope with frustrations at work and home on a daily basis based on the Word of God. They live in a home with eleven other men and learn to function as a family unit. Our goal is to raise Godly men for the future of our nation and our families. We are privileged to watch God change the hearts of these men and their families, time after time. We see God restore them first to Himself and then to their families.

After they graduate from Phase 1, they can participate in Phase 2, which is an extension of Phase 1. They follow all the same rules but are now allowed to work outside of ChristTown or go to school. If they do not have their High School diploma, we require them to get their GED while in Phase 2. During the second phase, they have the option to earn a degree or become certified in a trade, such as welding. Additionally, we assist them in restoring driver's licenses, paying debts, and obtaining transportation. We encourage them to stay and find work and save enough money to start fresh—on their own with Jesus!

Another key ingredient for their continued success is having their families start the recovery process, just as I did with Bob. To help the families accomplish this, we offer a series of Family Meetings. Anyone who wishes to be a part of the recovery process of their loved one needs to attend these meetings. Residents may take leave only with someone who has completed all four meetings. No loved ones are permitted to speak to a resident at church until they have attended the first meeting, at which we tell them about our program rules and strongly encourage them to respect these. The family meetings are patterned after the one that I attended at the Addiction Recovery Center. They are taught with the hope that the loved one will understand their need for a fresh start, too—with Jesus leading the way to the abundant life He died to give us! (John 10:10)

With all the amazing, exciting things that have happened over the years (more of those to come next chapter), there is nothing more inspiring than seeing a soul reconciled to God. With all the activities around ChristTown Ministries, we do our best to keep the main thing the main thing! We are here to do God's business, and His business is the people business! There is nothing more important than preaching the Good News, that in Christ we are new creations! We have a miracle-working God on our side Who empowers our ministry of reconciliation!

Chapter 7—Life In His Name

And they went out and preached everywhere, the Lord working with them and confirming the word through the accompanying signs. Amen.
Mark 16:20 NKJV

As one can imagine, the work done at ChristTown Ministries can often be challenging and unrewarding. All you need to do is a quick search on Google to discover the staggering drug and alcohol usage statistics. You will also find an astonishing number of people who die from addiction-related incidents. Only ten percent seek recovery treatment out of millions of people with addictions.[5]

Therefore, my beloved brethren, be steadfast, immovable, always abounding in the work of the Lord, knowing that your labor is not in vain in the Lord.
1 Corinthians 15:58 NKJV

We have been asked, "How successful is your program?" "100%!" is our standard reply. "Jesus and the Word are 100% successful if you follow His ways!"

---

[5] https://www.addictioncenter.com/addiction/addiction-statistics/

All for Jesus, Bob

Over the last twenty years of our ministry, I hate to say that we see more people return to their way and use drugs and alcohol rather than those staying clean and sober. I choose to dwell on 1 Corinthians 15:58 during these difficult and disappointing times. I also intentionally recall all the miracles I have seen God do at this little ministry in Quincy, Fl. And when I don't, the Lord will often send someone by to remind me of the work He is doing here!

And there are also many other things that Jesus did, which if they were written one by one, I suppose that even the world itself could not contain the books that would be written. Amen.
John 21:25 NKJV

Like John, we've experienced so many miracles that there is not enough time or paper to write about them all! I have chosen the following stories and testimonies so you can see the good, the bad, and the ugly of what we do. Mainly, I've chosen them so you can see the power of God at work in our lives and either come to believe that He still works miracles or maybe discover for the first time that He is still our miracle-working God! (Last names are withheld for the privacy of the program participants.)

DOUG

The following is a word-for-word testimony written by Doug on February 18, 2022:

"When I first came to know Bob Wells, I was a participant in a faith-based program located in downtown Tallahassee. The program was a rescue mission, a building owned by a large Baptist church also located in Tallahassee. I believe the rescue mission was funded mostly through the tithes of this "parent" church's congregants and truly was a wonderful help to me, but not quite enough. It was close to drugs—I was an addict and had been for twenty years.

Every Sunday, the men, including myself, were loaded into vans, up to twenty or thirty of us. Before the service, we headed to a Sunday school class. Bob Wells was our Sunday school teacher, and Laura Wells was there every Sunday singing in the choir. I only know this because Bob proudly let us know that was his beautiful wife up there singing.

And so, life in the program at the rescue mission was difficult for me. I truly was seeking the hand of God to rescue me from the pit that was my life. I would get so far in recovery, just far enough that friends and loved ones would begin to trust in and accept me again. Then I would crash.

Glenn Burns was the Director/Pastor of the program at the Rescue Mission. He had taken me under his wing and put much faith and confidence in me. After my second or third try to successfully complete this program, Glenn was ready to give me another try. I, however, was not. I knew in my heart that I would not be able to resist the temptation of drugs at that location. The location was in the center of a community eaten up with drug use. I told Glenn I needed to get away. I pleaded with him to help me find my sweet spot; the light I saw come into his eyes gave me hope. I knew God had given him my answer. He

All for Jesus, Bob

said he had a friend who had just basically given everything he had to start a program in Quincy, Florida. He asked me if this man would accept me would I be willing to go. I was.

Immediately Glenn got his friend on the line. It was Bob Wells. It was getting late in the evening, and to my surprise, Bob brought me into his home for the evening, saying he would get me set up in Quincy in the morning. He introduced me to Laura and their two children, Josh and Jackie Lee. He let me shower, fed me, and washed my clothes. Jackie Lee and Josh fought for my attention. Josh wanted to show off his new BB gun, and Jackie Lee wanted me to meet all her dolls. I honestly cannot say I have ever felt so welcome anywhere in all my life.

The next morning, we were all up early in a prayer circle with pillows on the floor. We held hands and prayed, and pastor Bob shared a Proverb. After that, we were fed, and I was whisked off feeling very blessed and hopeful to go to ChristTown Ministries in Quincy, Florida.

The Lord Jesus Christ came to redeem the lost, sick, oppressed, depressed, and afflicted, and he then uses the thankful new hearts of those same redeemed saints. The life of Bob and Laura Wells is a perfect example of how Christ Jesus is still alive today.

I sorely miss the huge hugs and holy kisses of Pastor Bob, for he has passed through my life and is now seated with Christ in the heavenly realm. But thank God the Jesus in him encouraged Miss Laura to continue the work He started in Pastor Bob and his wife, now Pastor Laura Wells.

I thank and love Miss Laura dearly for the love and strength she shows to all who care to see. She reveals a life filled with grace, mercy, and purpose to those who are willing to follow Jesus."

Doug is one of the first residents we were privileged to help. He has been in and out of the program several times, making his struggle with addiction over forty years. Doug readily admits the turmoil, loss, and hopelessness he experienced over the years is overwhelming. Choosing to not live in or dwell on his past, he is here now, sober and in his right mind fighting the good fight with God—truly allowing God to change him from the inside out. I find it very interesting that he is here on our twentieth anniversary, about to graduate Phase 1!

Can't you just feel the love of our God? The seeds of God's grace poured into Doug's life via ChristTown, and other ministries, have sprouted and are growing—to God be the glory! Doug stands as a shining example of how God's goodness and mercy follow us all the days of our lives! I am very thankful and delighted that Doug has finally stopped running, submitted to our Lord, and allowed the Lord to fill him with His mercy and change his life forever!

He has some deep wounds from his past—but God has given him hope for a future that can make a difference in others' lives! Today Doug's purpose in life is to share Christ and how He changed his life to youth. Doug has a deep desire to detour the youth from making the same mistakes he did and see them turn their lives over to Christ! We are looking forward to what God has for him in the next phase!

> *And let us not get tired of doing what is right, for after a while we will reap a harvest of blessing if we don't get discouraged and give up.*
> **Galatians 6:9 TLB**

JOE

We tease around here that Joe is our poster child for obtaining his GED and becoming certified in a trade. Joe's first attempt at recovery was a fail when he was with us for six months in 2012, but when he came back in 2015, he made a life-changing decision and allowed God access to every area of his life. He studied and did the hard work of applying what he learned in all the Bible classes, required reading, and Scripture memorization. While in

Phase 2, he studied and received his GED and attended Gadsden Technology Institute, where he completed the Welding Technology Technical Program. It took him just shy of four years, but today he is gainfully employed as a welder, living in his own place, driving his own car, paying his own bills, and praising Jesus for all his accomplishments!

CURTIS

When pushed to get his GED or go to work, Curtis wasn't happy with me. He was very upset and entertained thoughts of leaving and returning to his old lifestyle. The following is an excerpt from a letter he wrote to me after deciding to submit to the will of God for his life:

". . . with the tools, knowledge, and love that I was blessed with and given by this place that I call home (and how cool is it that it's called 'ChristTown'), I was freed even more. Sometimes I feel 'drunk' (ha-ha) at the fact that I get so excited at things that happen I can hardly contain myself. My hand and heart to God when I say I haven't been this content, almost even happy (which I am) in a very long time, 12 years, or thereabouts. I could finish this by listing the names of people who I believe helped make this possible, but this time, I am going just to tell it like it is—this is all about God and His kingdom, and all I can say is Praise Jesus, and I really do love you."

All for Jesus, Bob

In another letter:

"It's all God's work, but because of who I am, it's important for me to make it clear to you, Ms. Laura, we have had our differences in the past, but I can assure you that every single time I always learned something from you that always glorified God. So to me, you are one of the most important angels God is using to get me where I need to be with the soul prize at the end of this journey here . . . Heaven. Thank you for everything you do and provide, and I love you with the love of God . . ."

Curtis entered our program in 2014, and he stayed until 2015, left, and then came back in December of 2015. He received his GED in December of 2018. He moved to Heaven on April 9, 2020, at the age of 56. To God be the glory, Curtis leaves a legacy of the power of God in his changed life and the results of not quitting. The last part of his life leaves a shining testimony to others to forge through the emotions of not wanting to change, study, or do the next right thing. Instead of giving up—he kept doing the next right thing and found peace, love, contentment, and purpose! His parents lost their son, but they can be proud of what he accomplished, the legacy he left behind, and find solace that he is in Heaven with Jesus!

TYLER

Tyler came to our program straight from the County Jail. His first try was a short one, being here for only six months before he was caught with drugs and dismissed from the program. God had shown him mercy and moved on the judge's heart to sentence him to ChristTown instead of prison. After being arrested again, he stood before another judge, asking for a second chance, requesting to be sent back to ChristTown. God performed a miracle by turning the judge's heart right before his eyes, allowing Tyler to come to ChristTown again. He could have been sentenced to fifteen years in prison. In His abundant mercy, God sentenced him to ChristTown, including completing Phase 1 and Phase 2 of our program.

Tyler made it through Phase 1 and was attending TCC (Tallahassee Community College) for his GED, working as a paid employee on our moving truck, when temptation overcame him again, and he started using drugs. Yes, again, and while on our premises!

When this occurs, we are hurt and angry and feel betrayed. I said it this way because, unfortunately, he is not the only one that has done this or something similar over the years. Oh, the crazy things we've been through! Residents have stolen our vehicles, broke into our buildings, stolen stuff, bought drugs, and brought drugs to the house they purchased while they were out supposed to be doing ChristTown business. But praise belongs to God for the grace to be quick to forgive, let it go, and begin praying for them—asking God to line up circumstances that will turn them from their wicked ways and capture their hearts for His kingdom.

Tyler was dismissed from our program, which caused him to violate parole, triggering a warrant for his arrest. Currently, he is in prison doing the time he had the option to avoid and start a fresh new life with our awesome God. Pray for Tyler! Pray that he has a life-changing experience with God right now, right where he is.

KEVIN & THE SHULLAMITES

Kevin Shulla writes the following:

"It had finally occurred to me that something was missing. I had all the money and material things a man could want, and I was miserable! I talked to my employer at the time and told him I was struggling with pain pills that were prescribed to me. He offered to pay $30,000 for a three-month rehabilitation program, which I turned down because I didn't want him to bear the burden of my mistakes. As a compromise, I accepted his offer to take a month off paid. One of my brothers lived in Tallahassee and told me about ChristTown. So I came here and began to learn about who Christ is, what He had done, and how much He loved me. But, because of my past, I had a hard time believing He loved me, but I chose to stay past the thirty days my employer gave me off and stayed for three months. In a phone call to my wife at the time, she told me she had cancer and needed me to come home. Her mom died of cancer, and one of her sisters and two of her brothers, so needless to say, I split outta here to go back to help take care of her.

The next day after I returned to Sarasota, she had a doctor's appointment. She said she wanted to go alone, but I insisted that I go with her. I will never forget that moment when the doctor walked in and asked her, "What are you doing here? I told you it was benign." I realized then that I had made a mistake or, as we learn at ChristTown, I had taken the bait.

I called my boss to try and get my property management job back, and he apparently did his homework and knew I was in a year-long program. I lied to him and told him my wife had cancer, he told me to get my wife situated and get back to the drug & alcohol program, get a certificate and bring it back to me and you can have your properties back. If I wasn't so hard-headed and stubborn and just plain stupid, I should have realized that God had me in checkmate. But it took me two more years of pain & misery and finding out that rock bottom has a basement with a dungeon underneath it before I finally had enough.

At 2 am one morning, I cried out to God, and He heard my cry! The spot on my forehead where Miss Laura had previously placed anointing oil as she prayed over me two years prior started burning. The burning sensation turned into a warm sensation that went from my forehead to my soul, and a peace that I had never had before overwhelmed me, and I fell asleep. I woke up a couple of hours later and saw angels surrounding my bed. They had their backs to me with the whitest white feathers facing me. I fell back asleep, woke up, and knew that if I could just get back to ChristTown, I would be ok.

I will never forget hearing the sound of Pastor Bob's voice, which now I know was the sound of the Holy Spirit. He asked, "What's your deal?"

"My deal is, I've had enough! I have roots growing in me, and it feels like they are pulling me down to the pit of hell. Can you please come and get me?" I answered.

"If you want to come back here, we have a bed for you, but you will have to find a way to get here. You are five hours away, and we don't have a vehicle that will make it." We hung up.

All for Jesus, Bob

As I was getting high to keep from getting sick, I made phone calls to find a ride. I had burned through $169,000 and still had $14,000 left but couldn't rent a car because my license was suspended due to being arrested with possession of pills that were not prescribed to me. I couldn't drive because I was higher than Cooter Brown. My cousin from Chicago, a cop, flew down to drive me to ChristTown. Funny how God used a cop!

On our way to ChristTown, on I-75, I was being harassed in the back seat by voices saying, "$14,000, you'll blow that in a long weekend, you'll never amount to anything!" So I looked at my son sleeping peacefully, kissed him on the forehead, looked at the speed we were going, made sure we were in the center lane and made sure a semi was in the slow lane so if I didn't die when I hit the pavement the semi would finish the job. We were going 73mph. I heard the voice say, *"DO IT!"* I opened the door and jumped out so fast that my cousin said she didn't even realize what happened until her husband heard the semi blow his horn and saw me flying over the semi.

I can't remember too much of my past, but that moment is a time I remember everything like it just happened. The initial impact of my body hitting the concrete and launching me over the semi was not something I physically felt. Without a shadow of a doubt, I know it was one of the angels' wings that God surrounded me with when I cried out to Him that protected me. Call me crazy, and the state might agree, but I'm crazy for Christ and how He protected me.

Since then, making it back to ChristTown Ministries, my life hasn't been the same. I truly found everything I have been looking for, the missing piece of the puzzle, the void I lived with for so many years, has been filled by Jesus Christ—the only One who can fill it! (Colossians 2:10; Ephesians 2:10) There is so much more I could write and give detailed accounts of, but for the sake of time, paper, and space, the following is a list of just a few of the miracles He has done in my life with Scripture references to support He is Who He says He is!

He kept me alive when I jumped out of the car on I-75 at 73mph (Psalm 34:7; Psalm 91:11-12; Matthew 18:10 and Acts 12:9-15).

He allowed me to enjoy one last dinner with my brother, Curtis, who I had followed into drugs. He found Christ and he was a changed man. Curtis is one of the reasons I came to ChristTown. He used to text me Scripture all the time—I thought he was crazy! Some type of Jesus freak! We happened to be at his favorite restaurant for our last visit. He had told me about a race he ran in 49.9 seconds during this visit, which led him to Psalm 49:9. Shortly after our visit, he was killed in a tragic car accident. Knowing the sort of people that would be at his funeral service, protecting me from myself, Pastor Bob denied my request to go. I was angry, to say the least! The harassing thoughts began again—I was contemplating rebelling and running when I heard the still small voice of the Spirit of God say to me, "Psalm 49:9" I looked up that Scripture. It says *that he shall live forever and not see the pit.*[6]

What comfort these words brought to my aching heart—I cannot begin to describe the peace that flooded my mind and soul. This was the moment in my life when everything changed. I knew that I knew God had spoken to me and that He loved me. At this moment, I turned my life over to the care of Christ. Curtis' very last words to me were, "Just do the next right thing." These words were reinforced repeatedly here at ChristTown as I heard Pastor Bob say them all the time!

---

[6] Psalm 49:9 CSB

All for Jesus, Bob

Jesus didn't just save my life, but my whole family too! As Pastor Bob said, He went through the Shullamites like a white whirlwind! My brother Mike found the same new way of life here at ChristTown while Pastor Bob and Miss Laura cared for his daughter while he completed Phase 1. My father (who lived with me for the last five years of his life) experienced the love and peace here, and I was privileged to see him accept Jesus and have the most profound life change I've ever seen before he moved to Heaven in February of 2022. (Isaiah 54:13; Acts 16:31)

The Lord gave me my wife! (Genesis 2:18; Proverbs 18:22; Proverbs 31:10; Philippians 4:19; Proverbs 19:14; Psalm 37:4)

He restored my son to me! After the incident on I-75, the Department of Children and Family Services placed him in foster care—to God be the glory! Another checkmate by God that kept me here when I wanted to run! I knew I wouldn't be able to get him back—at least not the right way if I left. (Galatians 6:9)

God is using my wife and me to help build a church in another nation. (1 Peter 2:5; Acts 20:28; 1 Timothy 3:15; Haggai 1:8; Mark 16:15; Isaiah 55:1-13)

I am thankful for what God has done for me—the following Scriptures describe it: Jeremiah 29:11; Isaiah 40:29-31; Matthew 6:25-33; Proverbs 3:5-6; Philippians 4:6-7; Philippians 4:19!

He has strengthened me! He has given me rest! He takes care of ALL my needs! He answers my prayers—and when He doesn't, I trust that it's in my best interest! He has worked everything out for my good! He is always with me! He protects me, and I abide in the shadow of His wings! He has truly freed me from my sin and the bondage I put myself in! Oh, oh, oh, he who the Son sets free is free indeed! THANK YOU, JESUS!"

Kevin has been clean and sober at the time of this writing, just shy of eleven years! He is currently ChristTown's Associate Pastor! He not only heads up our moving business fundraising effort, but he also serves as our Men's Program Director. His brother, Mike, also is on staff at ChristTown; Mike is the Men's House Manager, works with his brother on the moving truck, and oversees the used furniture section of the thrift store. Kevin's life had undergone such a radical transformation that one of his brothers (the one he always looked up to) described him at the family gathering (when their father went to Heaven) as the family's spiritual leader.

> *Who through faith subdued kingdoms, worked righteousness, obtained promises, stopped the mouths of lions, quenched the violence of fire, escaped the edge of the sword, out of weakness were made strong, became valiant in battle, turned to fight the armies of the aliens.*
> **Hebrews 11:33-34 NKJV**

DYLAN, DERRICK, JIM, CALVIN & EARNIE

The list of names could go on! I feel like the writer of Hebrews, who, after listing several heroes of faith, started summing up speaking of prophets that through faith subdued kingdoms, worked righteousness, obtained promises, stopped the mouths of lions, and out of weaknesses were made strong! (Hebrew 11:33-34 NKJV)

Dylan had a profound life-changing experience with Jesus! While ministering the 7-Steps to Freedom in Christ to him, he surrendered and asked Jesus to become his Lord and Savior. He was restored to his family and received his AA Degree from Tallahassee Community College while here at ChristTown Ministries.

Derrick knew Jesus but had gotten off track. He re-surrendered his life to Christ, got his driver's license reinstated, got certified in digital media design from Gadsden Tech, and found work at a local furniture store.

Jim went through some tough life challenges during his first year at ChristTown, but we were blessed to see his heart change for Christ during Anger Management class! He was hired by a local company after completing Phase 1 and saved money for a vehicle, a deposit, and his first month's rent for an apartment. He is currently still working and living on his own.

Calvin completed his lengthy parole, served as Men's House Manager, reconciled with his family, and moved back to his hometown to start a well-digging business with his son.

Earnie was re-married to his wife and restored to children and grandchildren he didn't even know he had!

And truly Jesus did many other signs in the presence of His disciples, which are not written in this book; but these are written that you may believe that Jesus is the Christ, the Son of God, and that believing you may have life in His name.
John 20:30-31 NKJV

When we began ChristTown Ministries, Bob, Martha Ann, and I often prayed together for those we would be blessed to help. Our praying would often include that if all we did were for just one person to find what we had found in Christ, we would gladly do what He asked! We knew He would have died for us even if we were the only ones that needed His salvation—how could we not do for Him? Driven by our gratitude to Him, we gave Him our all. To Him be the glory—we have been fortunate to be eyewitnesses of these and many more life-changing experiences!

Additionally, we have experienced numerous financial and physical miracles! Homes and vehicles were donated at crucial moments. Large financial donations walked in the door, time and time again, at vital moments of urgent need! Maybe another book will be written regarding these, but for now—the stories included in this book provide a beautiful picture of God's purpose and what He does through ChristTown. The grace of God is transforming people's lives! I pray that these testimonies will cause you to believe that Jesus is the Christ, the Son of God, and that believing you would have life in His name!

Chapter 8—Choosing Joy

My brethren, count it all joy when you fall into various trials, knowing that the testing of your faith produces patience. But let patience have its perfect work, that you may be perfect and complete, lacking nothing.
James 1:2-4 NKJV

Bob and I used to kid each other that we should be the happiest people on the planet if we believed what James wrote! We also talked about writing a book about our journey. He would often throw out chapter titles, like, *Season of The Septics,* when we had several septic system failures happen in a row. Or, *Lawsuit Happy*, when we'd get a new legal notice in the long line of many from our neighbor or another entity. Or, *Financial Miracles*, as we continually watched in awe as our Jehovah-Jireh (The Lord our Provider) kept ChristTown and us personally afloat month after month when we had no clue how we would pay the bills. Or, *Broken Down Again,* when vehicles would constantly break down. Or, *Really?*, as we would experience one disappointment after another with residents turning their back on what God had to offer them and going back out for another run.

However, God sabotaged Satan's attempts to sabotage us! The enemy has (and still does) spent an enormous amount of time and energy in trying to derail ChristTown Ministries. With each trial, he was making his attempt to discourage and distract us from what God called us to do—make a difference in lives for the Kingdom of God. With each trial, God provided the answer, the way out, and the encouragement to keep on keeping on for Him. Bob's faith was solid and firm. He would often say, "Laura, there is no option B for me. I'm committed to Jesus and this ministry one hundred percent." And, of course, as you read in the last chapter, there were many, many victories along the way!

Whenever we were feeling discouraged, God always had someone come our way to give us a word of encouragement or let us know the impact ChristTown had made on their lives. Random people would call out of the blue, walk up to us in restaurants or parking lots—saying something similar to this, "I don't know you, and you don't know me, but God wanted me to come and tell you He's proud of you! Don't quit doing what you are doing for Him!" Or He might send us someone with whom we could retell our amazing journey, and in telling it, reliving all the incredible God-moments, our passion for continuing in the mission He has given us was renewed.

In 2014, several life-changing events occurred. The absolute highlight of that year was our son Joshua getting married in June to his precious wife, June. The wedding was the last my father would ever attend for our family, as cancer quickly took over his body and caused him to move to Heaven that November. We spent Thanksgiving laying him to rest.

At Christmas, while we were with my mom, I found out that Bob had been struggling with an issue with his throat for several months. The look from my sister (who is a DNP) after she looked at it said everything, *it was serious*, and we needed to get to a doctor as soon as possible. After having a biopsy done in January 2015, we heard the dreadful words, "it's cancer." Cancer would be the worst and the last of all the trials, troubles, and struggles we faced together.

All for Jesus, Bob

Before going to the doctor for a biopsy on his throat, Bob and I were having one of those conversations that you don't ever think you will have. "What if it is cancer? What will I do without you? How will the children navigate this? What will happen to ChristTown?" The stream of questions tumbled out of my mouth.

Again, Bob, the man of strong faith, responds, "If it is, the Lord will heal me. If He doesn't, I will be in Heaven, and He will be with all of you here, and you guys will be ok. And Laura, you can do ChristTown." "Not without you! I can't do life without you! We need you! No way! And—a woman running an all-male ministry? Surely God wouldn't ask me to do that!" was my reply. "Promise me, Laura, promise me that you will keep the ministry going." Bob pleaded with me. "Ok, I will, Bob. I promise to do my best to keep it going until God shows me who is to take it over."

I believe that Bob knew that he had cancer in July of 2014. When we were visiting my family over the 4th of July, he had spoken to my sister about the issue he was having with his throat, and she advised him to see a doctor. He was one hundred percent convinced that Jesus would heal him this side of Heaven, so he never went to see a doctor. He instead prayed and trusted Jesus, and not wanting to add to my heartache, he withheld all of this information from me because of what was happening with my father.

All for Jesus, Bob

When we returned home from the visit with my mom, we went to see an Ear, Nose, and Throat doctor. The goal was to verify what we were dealing with and then take it from there. They say hindsight is 20/20—if I could do anything over again, I would have kept Bob from having the biopsy done. I believe with my whole heart that that procedure sped up the growth of the cancer. Had the doctor told us before the procedure, what we heard after may have caused a change in getting the initial biopsy done. After the biopsy and an MRI, we went to see an oncologist for their plan on how to tackle the cancer.

Their plan was lots of chemotherapy and radiation; Bob would have spent an enormous amount of time in medical facilities and being very sick from the treatments. The growth in his throat was too large to have surgery, so the hope was to shrink it enough to make surgery a possibility. There was nothing they could do to cure Bob, and the measures they suggested would only *possibly* lengthen his days here. When we left, we were deeply disappointed. We felt nothing but death and despair in that place and said as much to each other. We drove home in silence, holding tightly to each other's hands.

All for Jesus, Bob

Rejoice always, pray without ceasing, in everything give thanks; for this is the will of God in Christ Jesus for you
1 Thessalonians 5:16-18 NKJV

Later that evening, Bob talked about what pained his heart the most telling— the children. We talked, prayed, and went to bed. The next morning after we both finished with our quiet time with the Lord, we came together to talk again about how we would face this trial. I shared with Bob what the Lord had spoken to me that morning, and he did likewise. We had both heard similar messages—*choose life, trust Me*. We both agreed that Bob would not go the traditional medical route for his healing but depend on God to heal him. We chose to trust Jesus and praying without ceasing took on a whole new meaning.

Full of faith, we began following God's plan for Bob's health; we next faced the most difficult part of the journey, telling the children. Naturally, each was devastated at the news. To understand their emotions, you would need to understand their relationships. Bob was a very large part of their lives; he always was, from the time they were born until he moved to Heaven.

The children were extremely close to him, and their relationships were real and intimate. Two of his three sons spoke to him daily at least once, if not multiple times per day. His other son wasn't daily but very often. Our daughter was a senior in High School and still at home. They were very close too. They fished together, she played softball, and they spent a lot of time practicing, and we were at the field every time she was on it. I am struggling with the words to describe his closeness to each of them. Father, best friend, advisor, and spiritual leader all come to mind—he was a colossal and important part of their lives. The gaping hole left by his absence still exists in all of our lives today. We've all been able to move forward—but we will never move on.

Initially, the tumor didn't stop Bob from his daily activities. We worked and attended our daughter's games and senior year activities, including her graduation. Bob changed his eating habits—started juicing and eating foods that would put his body in a high alkaline state. We prayed and spoke the Word of God over him every day, morning and evening. We held prayer meetings in our church where people would come and pray with and over him. We did everything we believed the Holy Spirit led us to do. The cancer kept growing, and so did the amount of pain he was in.

By August of 2015, Bob was in a mess. Being a recovered addict, the last thing he wanted to do was start taking narcotics, so he had been trying to manage his pain with ibuprofen and over-the-counter throat spray. On Friday evening, the 28th of August, after our daughter had gone to bed, Bob started puking large amounts of blood in a trash can and couldn't stop. I ran upstairs and woke Jackie to help me get her Dad out to the truck. He was incredibly weak, but we got him and the trash can up into our Excursion only by God's grace. We raced him to the emergency room, calling out to Jesus for help the whole way. Our youngest son, Joshua, met us there and helped us get him into the hospital. They got him stabilized and admitted him. The amount of ibuprofen he had been taking had caused stomach ulcers that began bleeding. His bleeding wasn't the only issue . . .

The cancer had grown and spread. It had wrapped itself around his esophagus and was literally choking the life out of him. We were faced with some major decisions.

All for Jesus, Bob

We were told that Bob most likely would not make it out of the hospital, but they wanted to do a tracheotomy to help him breathe. The procedure was for comfort measures only. We went ahead with the surgery and worked hard to manage the thought that he may never come home again. On our 25th wedding anniversary, which was the 1st of September 2015, we were in the hospital meeting with Pastor Ray to discuss funeral service arrangements for Bob. Not exactly what we had planned to be doing on our 25th. We'd been planning to travel the country together until about a week before he ended up in the hospital.

The look on his face and the tears in his eyes when he told me, "Honey, I don't think we will make our trip . . . I'm so sorry," will never leave me. I often tell couples now, don't put off doing things and spending time together . . . life is short. We said maybe next year so many times for our anniversary until we got close to the twenty-fifth when Bob started saying we were going. Next year may not come, so do it now!

Jackie was so thoughtful that day. She bought us cards to give to each other and a couple of bracelets for Bob to give me. The bracelets were cuff bangles with sayings on them. One said, *'You are My Person,'* and the other *'Choose Joy.'*

No longer drink only water, but use a little wine for your stomach's sake and your frequent infirmities.
1 Timothy 5:23 NKJV

After the surgery, we were faced with more major decisions. One of the main ones being, should he continue to take the narcotic pain medications? Much discussion and prayer went into that decision. Some friends and family were dead set against it, telling him not to give in to it and trust the Lord. Others wanted to see his pain alleviated. We ultimately concluded that God had a good use for these medications. We believed with all our hearts that it would be a temporary measure—either God would heal him of the horrid disease here on Earth, or Bob would be healed and with

All for Jesus, Bob

Jesus in Heaven. Either way—the drug use would be over, and he could find some relief here.

Unexpectedly, Bob got stronger, so they discharged us from the hospital and set us up for home Hospice care. Bob came home from the hospital and lived several more months. Again, it was ok at first; we found our new normal and adjusted to life with his tracheotomy. He went back to work and saw our son Joshua get pinned at his induction ceremony for the Tallahassee Fire Department. Eating became more of a challenge; his diet consisted of pureed meats and vegetables and meal replacement drinks. Hospice was coming once per week, his pain medication was low dosage, and we handled all of his other symptoms (of which I won't give you the gory details) pretty well. Amazingly he was still coming to work every day! Life settled into a 'new normal' routine until Christmas Eve of 2015 when he took a major turn for the worse.

One of his favorite things to do was pass out stockings to all the men in the program and those that attended our Christmas Eve service. He was blessed to do that one last time. After passing them out, he told me he needed to get home; he was tired. A couple of hours later, he was in unbearable pain. I called Hospice, but they didn't get there until early Christmas morning. We could barely endure the hours it took for them to arrive—he was suffering so much. That Christmas was a sad one for us all—he was there but not really because of the medication he was on, and we all knew the situation had gone from bad to worse. The reprieve we'd felt after leaving the hospital in September was over.

> *God is our refuge and strength,*
> *A very present help in trouble.*
> **Psalm 46:1 NKJV**

I watched his health deteriorate, and my heart broke. My strong, invincible father was taken by cancer, and now I watched helplessly the love of my life being taken the same way. The sadness physically hurt at times—yet there existed a strength and a calm inside our home and lives. We just knew that everything was going to be ok.

The Hospice nurse or my sister would tell me about things that may happen to Bob and what to watch for, and they explained how to use the pieces of equipment they had brought to help him through those times. Things that would keep him from suffocating, choking, or being unable to breathe. I would think *that's not going to happen*—and of course, it did! If they said this is the worst thing that could happen, it happened. I am so grateful today for how God guided us both through these very difficult days. He gave us the ability to handle and do things that we never thought we could—and truly could not withstand without His power. God's grace gave us the power to do things we never thought we would be doing in a million years.

Once again, I had a very keen sense of Christ working through me, of His literal presence in our times of distress. The depth of love and peace in our home was immeasurable. The ability He gave me to care for Bob and meet his needs is nothing short of a miracle. Bob's faith and trust were extraordinary. Our Lord's love for us is limitless, and He truly never leaves nor forsakes us. He is our ever-present help in time of need. Again, I will spare you the gorier details of what he went through. Suffice it to say; I would not wish it upon my worst enemy. I will forever be grateful to Jesus for seeing us through the valley of death.

We spent the last two months of his life in the Hospice House. Just when they thought they had him stabilized and were about to send him home, something would happen that kept him there. This turned out to be a blessing as he did not want to die in our home, and the care he was given there was incredible. It is an additional miracle that his medical needs were met financially and physically.

Those last two months, I left his side on only two occasions. Once to go home and supervise the living room getting ready for an anticipated arrival, and the other to vote in the presidential primary. His sister Martha stayed with him both times, so I had a small peace that he was not alone. The children came by almost daily, and others came to visit, but we mostly did not receive visitors—it was just too hard.

> *So it was that the beggar died and was carried by the angels to Abraham's bosom.*
> *The rich man also died and was buried*
> **Luke 16:22 NKJV**

Bob took his last breath here on Monday, the 14th of March 2016. Scripture teaches us that angels escort us to Heaven, and I unquestionably believe it. I am certain that

Bob's escort was above and beyond anything that he could have ever imagined, and I would love to say that this was a beautiful experience this side of Heaven, but it wasn't. It was ugly, painful, and heartbreaking. My daughter explained it best; those last two months we were waiting for him to leave us felt like we were standing at the edge of a cliff waiting for someone to push us off—we just didn't know when or what it would be like. That day we discovered the shock and pain of being pushed into a dark, dismal abyss. I vaguely remember making it through the motions of having his body picked up by the funeral director and getting back to the house.

> *But He was wounded for our transgressions,*
> *He was bruised for our iniquities;*
> *The chastisement for our peace was upon Him,*
> *And by His stripes, we are healed.*
> **Isaiah 53:5 NKJV**

I wish I could say that I had the same faith as Bob. I will tell you plainly; Bob died the way he lived, full of faith! He would often say, "I'm in a win-win situation! I will be healed and get to stay here, or I will be healed and be in eternity with Jesus!" I recall vividly waking up sobbing, alone in our bed the morning after he moved to Heaven, thinking, "What will I do? How will I navigate life without you, Bob? How in the world will I be or do any good for the men at ChristTown? Why, why am I here, God, and

Bob is not? It sure seems that it should be the other way around."

Then, despite my sobs, I heard Bob's voice saying something I'd heard him say many times before, "When you don't know what to do, you can't go wrong doing right, so just do the next right thing." My soul flooded with peace. Laying there, I asked, "God, what is my next right thing to do? *"Be in the pulpit tomorrow evening. The people need to hear from you,"* was His reply.

As I said earlier, I hadn't left Bob's side for two months, so that meant both he and I had been away from the ministry for that length of time. We communicated with Martha Ann the whole time via phone and visits but were not there in their physical presence. I immediately understood what God was saying to me. I got up out of bed and got into the Word of God. If I am going to deliver a Word from Him, I need to study, pray and prepare for it.

God is so good! He knew exactly what I needed; I needed Him and His Word. If I had not had the accountability, I honestly don't know if that's where I would have gone—I was so angry at God. My routine for the next year or so became getting up, getting in the Word, and asking God what my next right thing to do was—then going and doing it.

All for Jesus, Bob

We buried Bob in Beachton, Georgia, on the 17th of March 2016. His celebration of life service held many more miracles. There had to have been at least six hundred people in the church that morning. Bob's oldest son Dustin spoke, and Pastor Ray delivered the message of the Gospel just as Bob had asked him to. We praised the Lord for His goodness and mercy towards us and the hope we had of seeing Bob again one day. Pastor Ray said some words that day that has helped me a little with my "Why did this have to happen to Bob?" question. Had Bob died when he was eighty or ninety, many of the people there that morning might not have been there to hear the Good News. Many people there accepted Jesus as their Savior that day, and many others re-dedicated their lives to Him!

To console those who mourn in Zion,
To give them beauty for ashes,
The oil of joy for mourning,
The garment of praise for the spirit of heaviness;
That they may be called trees of righteousness,
The planting of the Lord, that He may be glorified.
Isaiah 61:3 NKJV

All for Jesus, Bob

Bob's death was horrible. We wanted so badly for God to heal him here. I wanted to grow old with him. Jackie wanted him to see her get her Master's Degree and walk her down the aisle when she married her amazing husband Mabry. We would have given anything for Bob to be here for the birth of Josh and June's first child, Waylon Robertson, and any future children Josh and Jackie would have. The grandchildren didn't want to lose their Grandpa. The grief at moments has torn our family apart and our hearts to pieces. The loss was and is huge. Our lives will never be the same.

As I struggled through those days after Bob moved, I learned that I had a choice. My heart held two distinct emotions, grief, and joy. Bob and I focused on what we wanted to happen here—God wants our focus on Him there in Heaven. It was my choice to decide which I would live in each day. Would I accept Jesus' offer? Would I trade Him my mourning for His oil of joy? Nearly every day that first year I would put on the bracelet I received on our 25th wedding anniversary. By God's grace and power, as I walked out the door each morning, I spoke to Him aloud, "Father, today I choose Joy."

All for Jesus, Bob

Chapter 9—Walking Through

> *Blessed are those who mourn,*
> *For they shall be comforted.*
> **Matthew 5:4 NKJV**

The pain I experienced was (and at times still is) excruciating—my suffering and loss indescribable. I traveled through the worst fog and aching I've ever been through. My faith was rattled deeply. When Bob moved, I had to deal with many earthly challenges . . . like the truck not starting, waking up with my tub full of septic sewage, and estate issues that we thought we had handled properly, only to find out the day after he died, we didn't. Not to mention taking over ChristTown Ministries, family concerns, and helping others deal with their grief from losing their father, friend, and Pastor. My life was full of thorns and nettles, challenges, and trials—suffering and loss. And I was angry.

My son, give attention to my words; Incline your ear to my sayings. Do not let them depart from your eyes; Keep them in the midst of your heart; For they are life to those who find them, And health to all their flesh.
Proverbs 4:20-22 NKJV

God be glorified, He had me up each morning and in His Word. If I wasn't studying to prepare for a Wednesday or Sunday message, I read the Proverb for the day. I remember clearly the day I read Proverbs chapter 4. After reading verses twenty to twenty-two, shown above, "OH YEAH? THIS DIDN'T WORK FOR BOB!" Holding the pen in my hand as if ready to stab someone with it, I ripped through several pages of the Bible as I wrote those words.

The anger that flowed from my heart was deep and immense. I would yell at God, "You were the One that said instead of doing radiation and chemotherapy, I should pray over him. Choose life. Trust You."

"Your Word says, by Your stripes, we are healed! That didn't work for Bob!"

"You said that those that placed their trust in You would NEVER be disappointed—well, I am! We prayed, we trusted and look where that got us! Bob is dead! BOB IS DEAD! I did what You asked and it didn't work! We did our part; You didn't do Yours!"

All for Jesus, Bob

I am so embarrassed, and my heart wrenches at the thought of how I spoke to God. I would even like to say that this was a one-time thing, but it wasn't. Being rawly honest, I knew He had the power to heal Bob, and He chose not to. I, in my audacity, felt God *owed* us. We had done so much for Him, and He didn't come through in our greatest moment of need. Staying in His Word revealed my incorrect thinking . . .

> *You never saw him, yet you love him. You still don't see him, yet you trust him—with laughter and singing. Because you kept on believing, you'll get what you're looking forward to: total salvation.*
> **1 Peter 1:8-9 MSG**

A friend of mine had given me a couple of books when she came for Bob's funeral. One of them was Randy Alcorn's book called **Heaven**. The first year after Bob moved to Heaven, I read that book at his graveside. I would give the Sunday morning message, leave the church, and drive to Georgia, where Bob's grave was. I'd set up a chair, take my umbrella with me (because it was blazing hot and no shade), cry, read, and talk to Bob and Jesus. Reading this book, I discovered many incredible truths about Heaven! My view had been so distorted I realized I was not looking forward to going there! While reading this book weekly, I was also studying the cross.

The Lord had led me to get back to the basics, and I taught a series of lessons from the sayings on the cross.

And about the ninth hour Jesus cried out with a loud voice, saying, "Eli, Eli, lama sabachthani?" that is, "My God, My God, why have You forsaken Me?
Matthew 27:46 NKJV

Be anxious for nothing, but in everything by prayer and supplication, with thanksgiving, let your requests be made known to God; and the peace of God, which surpasses all understanding, will guard your hearts and minds through Christ Jesus.
Philippians 4:6-7 NKJV

The question "Why?" bothered me until God spoke to me during a lesson I prepared and one I received from a visiting pastor. Jesus asked the Father and the Holy Spirit, "Why?" As He hung on the cross, His cries hung in the air unanswered with words. His answer lay in what He was doing. He was paying the price for our sin, mine and yours, so we wouldn't have to. He was making the way for us to be with Him in Heaven for eternity. He loves us with indescribable love and gives us the gift of total salvation through our belief in His death and resurrection.

Philippians 4 tells us that the peace that passes all understanding will guard our hearts and minds through

All for Jesus, Bob

Christ Jesus as we pray. Pastor Isa (the visiting pastor) emphasized that we must move past understanding to get to peace. These words exploded in my heart, and I was comforted. The *why* was for the sake of the Kingdom—and if God the Father could accept the death of His One and only Son for the salvation of souls, who was I not to accept the same? People were redeemed at Bob's funeral. God had chosen to use Bob's life to impact souls for eternity. I have chosen not to try and figure out the why anymore. I no longer question—I choose to trust.

I received enormous peace discovering what Heaven was like and envisioning things that Bob was most likely doing there. At the end of the year and the book, God began to speak to me regarding moving forward. He gave me the following passage of Scripture:

"Do not fear, for you will not be ashamed;
Neither be disgraced, for you will not be put to shame;
For you will forget the shame of your youth,
And will not remember the reproach of your
widowhood anymore.
For your Maker is your husband,
The Lord of hosts is His name;
And your Redeemer is the Holy One of Israel; He is
called the God of the whole Earth.
For the Lord has called you Like a
woman forsaken and grieved in spirit,
Like a youthful wife when you were refused," Says
your God. "For a mere moment I have forsaken you,
But with great mercies I will gather you.
With a little wrath I hid My face from you for a
moment; But with everlasting kindness
I will have mercy on you,"
Says the Lord, your Redeemer.
Isaiah 54:4-8 NKJV

"Fear not, Laura—you will no longer live in shame. Don't be afraid there is no more disgrace for you. You will no longer remember the shame of your youth or the sorrow of widowhood. For your Creator will be your Husband; the LORD of Heavens Armies is His name! He is your Redeemer, the Holy One of Israel, the God of all the Earth. For the Lord has called you back from your grief—as though you were a young wife abandoned by her husband, says your God." I heard Him say through the passage of Scripture found in Isaiah 54:4-8 NKJV.

I was humbled beyond measure as He filled my heart anew with hope and a desire to lead others to have life-changing encounters with Him. His power, the Holy Spirit in me, regenerated my lifeless heart. Being in the Word day after day glued the pieces of my broken heart back together, reviving the passion for life and His Word that had slipped away from me in Bob's illness and departure.

God is my Husband! He encouraged me to take my focus off of what I didn't have and put it on what I did have. Speaking to my heart, He said, "Bob was yours for a season, but He's completely mine now. You have your children, family, and the ministry." It was time to move forward. He wanted me to stop coming to the graveside. God assured me, "Bob is with Me! He is alive! I AM here, Laura, I AM real, I AM your God, your Maker, your Husband, your Power, your power to endure. Look to Me; I Am the Author and Finisher of your faith. We've more work to do . . ."

All for Jesus, Bob

God and I reviewed the previous year as I stood there at Bob's graveside for what I knew would be the last time for an undetermined amount of time. He showed me all the amazing things He had accomplished through my submission to Him and following His lead to the next right thing to do each day. To God be all the glory—He did all of it even though I was very angry with Him for most of the year for taking Bob from me. What love! What a Savior! He did through me what I could not do for myself.

On my birthday (November 14, 2016), my children gave me a bracelet that was engraved with Bob's handwriting. One side said, "heart & soul" and the other said, "forever yours." ("I love you heart & soul" was how Bob would sign his cards & texts to us.) It was in the moment that I read the words "forever yours" that the Holy Spirit spoke to me and said he is not yours anymore—he is Mine.

Recalling my tirade about Bob being dead, He assures me again, "Bob's not dead. He's fully alive. He is with Me."

My heart aching, I acknowledged the truth of what He had just spoken to me. I was given the gift of Bob for almost 30 years, and now he was with the One he truly belonged to, Jesus. In his book, **Heaven**, Randy Alcorn talks about us not truly finding our Happily Ever After until we reach our destination of eternity with Jesus; when I read that, an overwhelming sense of earthly loss

All for Jesus, Bob

yet heavenly hope overtook me. Bob was living his happily ever after; mine is yet to come.

The curriculum we teach at ChristTown has also had an incredible impact on my life. When I teach, I get to take. What I mean is that every time I teach **Anger Management** or minister the **7 Steps to Freedom In Christ**, or **Enemies of the Heart**, I too am taking the class. I study to teach, and the Lord ministers to me as I study! **Enemies of the Heart** is where I discovered that I felt God owed me. In **Anger Management**, we learn that anger stems from unmet needs; I definitely had an unmet need! I needed Bob to be with me! In each class, but especially in the **7 Steps to Freedom In Christ**, I am reminded that I need to forgive to maintain my peace and joy. I need to cancel debts and trust that God truly does supply all of my needs.

All for Jesus, Bob

"Unforgiveness is like drinking poison yourself and waiting for the other person to die."
-Marianne Williamson

Am I saying that I needed to forgive God? Yes, that is exactly what I am saying! When we understand what forgiveness is—we understand that forgiveness is not about the other person. God didn't need my forgiveness. Unforgiveness is like taking poison every day and hoping the other person dies. I needed to forgive so my heart would be right! I need to quit taking the poison!

Additionally, **Anger Management** teaches us the many facets of anger. Frustration, loneliness, depression, sadness, and desire to quit are facets of anger. We all experience these emotions, and I am blessed to be able to teach a class that teaches me how to manage them positively. I experience these and many more as I navigate all the trauma and dramas that arise with the type of work we do here at ChristTown, and as I experience personal family difficulties. The hurts, betrayals, and disappointments bring about negative feelings, but when I take them to Jesus, He allows me to cast them upon Him, which alleviates the weight from myself.

All for Jesus, Bob

Do not sorrow, for the joy of the Lord is your strength.
Nehemiah 8:10b NKJV

Resilience is the capacity to recover quickly from difficulties.[7] Being able to preach a message the Wednesday after Bob moved to Heaven and navigating my way through work every day speaks of the resilience in my life. I hope you see clearly where my resilience comes from! I found strength in the Word of God every day as I spent time with Him. I spent time with God at Bob's graveside, on long walks, or riding my bicycle around the lake where I lived at the time. I listened to Christian music, the Bible, and other preachers. As ChristTown required our residents to speak the Word of

---

[7] https://www.google.com/search?q=resilience+definition

God over their lives, I did the same—reminding myself of who I am in Christ. I cried, prayed, lamented, shouted in anger, and praised simultaneously—and God loved me through it all. He comforted me, guided me, and gave me the strength to do the next right thing.

Another saying Bob had was, "What you feed will lead!" I fed my soul positive, uplifting things, and God led me to a place of peace and joy.

> *The thief does not come except to steal, and to kill, and to destroy. I have come that they may have life, and that they may have it more abundantly.*
> **John 10:10 NKJV**

I am deeply grateful for where God placed me and my responsibilities because it keeps me immersed in His Word and my heart right before Him. We live in a sin-sick world, there will always be trials, troubles, and negative situations in our lives, but we have the power to overcome it all! The thief comes to steal, kill, and destroy, but the Lord said He came to give us life! (John 10:10) In this world, we will have trials and tribulations Jesus told us, but we could be of good cheer and even joyful because He has overcome them all! (John 16:33) The word life in John 10:10 can be translated as the power to endure! He has given *me* the power to endure and the power to endure in abundance.

The God-given power of forgiveness is the source of my resilience! God-given grace is the source of my resilience! Seeing God work miracles in the lives of the men here at ChristTown and in my own life brings joy—and the joy of the Lord is, without a doubt, my strength!

> *Yea, though I walk through the valley of the shadow of death, I will fear no evil; For You are with me; Your rod and Your staff, they comfort me.*
> **Psalm 23:4 NKJV**

Psalm 23:4 says, though I walk *through* the valley, we don't pull over and park in it! His rod and staff comfort us—even when we are angry. We could replace the word staff for a walking stick; God is our walking stick! We lean on Him and He guides our every step. Until the day I get to move from here to Heaven, I will continue to choose joy because I know I am just walking through.

All for Jesus, Bob

Chapter 10—All For Jesus, Bob

Anyone who belongs to Christ is a new person.
The past is forgotten, and everything is new.
1 Corinthians 5:17 CEV

I continually stand in awe of seeing God take a life that was literally living for Satan, causing all kinds of havoc and transforming it into one full of peace and contributing to society. Bob's sobriety journey started in 1996, but after several years people found it hard to believe that he had ever done anything but serve the Lord. They couldn't picture him as a drug addict! The way he lived his life was large and filled with love. His respect from friends, family, and the community was nothing short of a miracle! His life is a reflection of 1 Corinthians 5:17! His past was forgotten—everything in his life was new! God pulled us out of the pit and set us on solid ground. Our past is just that—past! It doesn't define who we are—God does!

It's a lot easier to go through hell with Jesus than to Hell without Him!" -Pastor Bob

Even though we've been through many fiery trials, I would not trade places with anyone, and I know if Bob were here, he would say the same thing! Bob used to say, "It's a lot easier to go through hell with Jesus than to hell without Him!" Live for Jesus—it is worth it! As we end our time together, I want to tell you some more personal, incredible awesome things that occurred because we served God radically.

> *whom having not seen you love. Though now you do not see Him, yet believing, you rejoice with joy inexpressible and full of glory,*
> **1 Peter 1:8 NKJV**

Joy unspeakable. The word joy in 1 Peter 1:8 is chara which means cheerfulness, which is calm delight. This word comes from the primary word chairo. To have chairo is to be full of cheer, calmly happy, or well off. You could say chairo to someone as you are leaving their company, and it would be saying, "be well."[8] There was always a calm delight through every trouble, stress, and trial—even amidst my apprehensions and fears. We just had the knowing deep in our spirit that everything would be alright. Our Lord promised that everything would work out for good and His glory—we believed and have experienced it.

---

[8] Strong, S.T.D., LL.D., James. *Strong's Exhaustive Concordance of the Bible*. Public Domain, 1890.

All for Jesus, Bob

Joshua. Through his time with ChristTown, Joshua became an extremely good guitarist! Bob bought him his first guitar when he was around ten years old. He learned to play by watching the men who played on the praise team and, of course, practiced a lot at home. He also became a very proficient drummer! He would go into the church, turn on music, and play along on the drums! More importantly, Joshua was given compassion for people and wanting to help—he currently serves as a firefighter with the Tallahassee Fire Department and a guitarist on the praise team at his church. His experience working with addicts and the less fortunate gives him great insight into many of the calls he responds to while on the job. He's also written a few songs that still stir people's hearts to worship today.

Jackie. Jackie also played the drums. Her story, however, is a little different. We needed a drummer because the one we'd had for a while had left, so we asked her to sit down at the drums and see what happened. She ended up playing them for the next eight years! Again, more importantly, she was also given compassion for people. Especially the children of the less fortunate. She always desired to become a teacher—she currently serves as a Special Educator at an elementary school in Tennessee.

Both of our children were eyewitnesses to many victories and defeats—but to God be the glory in the end, I couldn't think of a better way to raise them than serving God by loving and helping His people, all to His glory.

Provision. Our family never went without anything. We were concerned at times with how we would do things financially, but God always saw us through. They both attended a Christian grade school and high school. Joshua's fire school was paid for. Jackie's college was paid for with her walking away with just a few thousand dollars in student loans. We always had a roof over our heads, clothes on our backs, and food on the table—but most importantly, we had God and His love at the center of our lives.

Wisdom. James 1:5 says that if we lack wisdom, all we need to do is ask, and God will give it to us liberally! I have experienced time and time again where I had no clue how to do something, and God showed me! The first time I had this very profound experience with God was when I needed to set up an accounting system to keep track of our finances. We bought QuickBooks, and I had no clue how to use it! So, I took my computer home with all the paperwork I needed and set it up at the kitchen table. Monday morning, I sat down at the table and prayed, "God, You said if we needed wisdom, all we needed to do was ask. I am asking You to show me how to set up our accounting system and use this software You've blessed us with." By Friday, the system was set up! We are still using this same format today!

I cannot tell you how many conversations He has led for me, the decisions He has made, and teaching me how to do things in which I have no college learning or experience! I stand as a personal witness to affirm—yes, he gives wisdom liberally!

Return to the stronghold, You prisoners of hope. Even today I declare That I will restore double to you.
Zachariah 9:12 NKJV

This I recall to my mind, Therefore I have hope. Through the Lord's mercies we are not consumed, Because His compassions fail not
Lamentations 3:21-22 NKJV

Now may the God of hope fill you with all joy and peace in believing, that you may abound in hope by the power of the Holy Spirit.
Romans 15:13 NKJV

Hope. I am a prisoner of Hope! I believe and count on His mercies being new every morning! Yes, I have losses, struggles, fears, and worries—but I choose to focus on the goodness and great mercy of our Lord, and hope abounds in my soul!

I pray that ChristTown Ministries will continue sharing this hope for generations! That ChristTown will continue to be a safe place to come to. I pray men will hear in their hearts—*if I can just get to ChristTown, I know I will be ok.* I pray that hope and vision will be restored in their lives. I pray their families would be reconciled. I pray that they will become the men God intended them to be! We need godly men, godly fathers in our homes and country! I pray that ChristTown Ministries will continue to show that our Jesus is in the life-changing business! That He rescues and saves! Bob used to say, "If I could just get them to fall in love with Jesus, they will be ok wherever they go, wherever life leads them, and through whatever life throws at them." I pray that men would fall in love with Jesus, be changed, and become life-changers in our world.

All for Jesus, Bob

If then you were raised with Christ, seek those things which are above, where Christ is, sitting at the right hand of God. Set your mind on things above, not on things on the earth.
Colossian 3:1-2 NKJV

Let us take our eyes off all that is here in front of us, the good and the bad, and place them on Christ! It is through knowing who we are in Christ and following His Word that lives are completely transformed. Jesus is the answer. He is the answer to all of life's issues—addictions, bad marriages, straying children, financial problems, worries, stresses, loss, broken relationships, or any other hardship you are facing.

These little troubles are getting us ready for an eternal glory that will make all our troubles seem like nothing
2 Corinthians 4:17 CEV

As they say, if you want to walk on water—you gotta get out of the boat! Even though we experienced deep sorrow, we've also experienced God on a level that I never knew existed. If you have any inkling whatsoever to serve radically—do it! Any troubles that come are light and momentary compared to the joy! Step out, and don't miss out on the enormous blessings He has. True, we have suffered a lot, but they will soon seem like nothing! Plus—the peace and joy we have right now, today, is off the chain. The stability of our everyday life is a direct result of where we are standing! We stand on solid ground—we stand on the Rock, Jesus Christ!

So we're not giving up. How could we! Even though on the outside it often looks like things are falling apart on us, on the inside, where God is making new life, not a day goes by without his unfolding grace. These hard times are small potatoes compared to the coming good times, the lavish celebration prepared for us. There's far more here than meets the eye. The things we see now are here today, gone tomorrow. But the things we can't see now will last forever.
2 Corinthians 4:16-18 MSG

Pastor Bob would tell you, "If He can transform my life, He can transform yours too! Give Him a try! Just give Him a year, do everything He asks, and see if your life isn't much better!"

All for Jesus, Bob

I couldn't think of a better way to end this book than with words from Pastor Bob himself. Pastor Bob wrote the following for a newsletter we sent out in 2003:

September 30, 2003

To His Dearest- The Body,

My bride asked me to put together a "short" testimony for our most recent newsletter. For me to put together anything "short" stating what our most gracious Lord & Savior Jesus has done in my life would be impossible. I promise you I will be as brief as possible!

All for Jesus, Bob

First, I need to introduce myself, my name is Bob Wells and I am a "major-league" sinner saved by a much more "MAJOR-LEAGUE GRACE." Many years ago, at the age of 12, I made Jesus my Savior. It wasn't until many years later that I finally made Him Lord of my life. And Oh! What a Lord He is!!!

He rescued me back in 1996 from a major addiction to alcohol, narcotics, & cocaine. My life was nothing but a path of destruction for myself and all those in my "wake," which I'm sorry to say that many were influenced and affected by my erratic self-pleasing lifestyle. After a couple of near-death episodes from overdoses, etc. I found myself on June 16th, 1996, "Fathers Day," in a room on the 3rd floor of Tallahassee Community Hospital detoxing. Finally, for the first time in my life, I felt as though I had come to the end of myself and began seeking guidance from my real Father, Our Lord, and Creator.

Little did I realize how true His Word would ring, "Call unto Me and I will answer you, and show you great and mighty things, which you do not know." Being at my end, I found His beginning, and how marvelous it was to step out of darkness into the Light!

As my appetite for His Word and His Way grew over the next few years, I threw myself into His arms in reckless abandonment, knowing He was preparing me as a vessel

All for Jesus, Bob

for His chosen purpose, I knew life as I had previously known (self-seeking) was over and would now be given wholly to His service. On November 25, 2001, sitting on the church pew, He clearly told me, "I want you to serve me full time"! Upon getting home from church that day, I told my wife He has called and I have answered, "Yes! Here I am send me!" She asked, "where and to what"? I said, "I don't have a clue but, just as He has been preparing me, He has also been preparing a ministry for me, which He will reveal in His time."

On August 1, 2002, ChristTown Ministries began in Quincy, Florida. Wow! What a journey this has been, an incredible year of "walking by faith, and not by sight." We seldom are allowed to see very far down the road. He is training us not to be an independent people but a God-Dependent people.

When God called me to begin this ministry, we knew it was going to require the sacrifice of self, time, comfort, and money. After praying for the Lord's direction, we put our home and property up for sale, went to the bank and took out a line of credit for $100,000.00, and began leasing a property that consists of a 23-unit motel, a 22,000 sq. ft. warehouse, and a 12-room boarding house. We are privileged to house women and children in the hotel and men in the boarding house. We hold chapel services and are planning to open a thrift store in the warehouse as soon as we have the funding to meet the building & fire code requirements, etc.

Needless to say, a ministry such as this is quite a financial load each month, and during the times when we were wondering how we were going to make it, the Lord always faithfully called one of His children to step up and help bear the burden. We are running an average cost of about $12-15,000.00 per month, with no salaries being paid whatsoever. Everyone working to meet the needs, whether full or part-time, is strictly on a volunteer basis.

I am once again, as has been many times on this journey, coming to the end of myself, which is always a good and exciting thing! Because this is when the Master can step forward and show His Majesty. We are at the end of our line of credit; our property and home are under contract to be closed by the end of December, which will give us some much-needed cash flow to help secure ownership of property for ChristTown Ministries vs. leasing property. Many times during prayer and speaking with brothers and sisters in Christ, the Lord has said to me, "You have not because you ask not" as humbly as I can, I am asking you, His body, to please help. All I ask is for you to pray and seek direction from Him, do as He leads.

Many, many souls have been saved, literally thousands of meals fed, and much love abounded. I suppose one of the greatest blessings to see, besides a lost soul coming

All for Jesus, Bob

into the saving knowledge of our Lord Jesus, is to see a hardened, fearful child come into a life of stability and love and to burst out of the hard shell the world has caused him/her to place around themselves and become a true child again full of smiles, laughter, and hugs, learning once again I can trust, things can be different! We truly must rescue the perishing and care for the dying! The field is white with harvest, but the laborers are few.

All for Jesus,

Bob

All for Jesus, Bob

Trust in the Lord with all your heart,
And lean not on your own understanding;
In all your ways acknowledge Him,
And He shall direct your paths.
Proverbs 3:5-6 NKJV

All for Jesus, Bob

All for Jesus, Bob

About the Author

Laura J. Wells left a successful career in the mortgage business to co-found ChristTown Ministries, Inc. (www.ChristTown.org) with her husband Bob Wells and his sister Martha Ann Wells.

ChristTown, born in 2002, is a ministry dedicated to changing the direction of men's lives from death to life through teaching them Christ-centered living.

Since her husband Bob moved to heaven in 2016, she has been serving as ChristTown's Pastor/Director. Her journey through addiction with Bob and their radical transformation by following the Word of God will unquestionably inspire you.

Laura is the author of **Trees of Righteousness: Living and Lasting Evidence of God,** a 10-Week in-depth Bible Study of Isaiah 41:17-20. She is passionate about the Word of God and helping people live the life Jesus died for them to live.

All for Jesus, Bob

Bibliography

Scripture quotations marked TPT are from The Passion Translation®. Copyright © 2017, 2018 by Passion & Fire Ministries, Inc. Used by permission. All rights reserved. ThePassionTranslation.com.

Scripture quotations marked NLT are taken from the Holy Bible, New Living Translation, Copyright © 1996, 2004, 2015 by Tyndale House Foundation. Used by permission of Tyndale House Publishers, Inc., Carol Stream, Illinois 60188. All rights reserved.

Scripture quotations marked NKJV are taken from the New King James Version®. Copyright © 1982 by Thomas Nelson. Used by permission. All rights reserved.

Scripture quotations marked KJV are taken from the King James Version.

Scripture quotations marked NIV are taken from The Holy Bible, New International Version®, NIV® Copyright© 1973, 1978, 1984, 2011 by Biblica, Inc.® Used by permission. All rights reserved worldwide.

Scripture quotations marked CEV are taken from the Contemporary English Version®,

Copyright © 1995 American Bible Society. All rights reserved.

Scripture quotations marked MSG are taken from The Message. Copyright © 1993, 1994, 1995, 1996, 2000, 2001, 2002. Used by permission of NavPress Publishing Group.

Scripture quotations marked TLB are taken from The Living Bible, copyright © 1971 by Tyndale House Foundation. Used by permission of Tyndale House Publishers Inc., Carol Stream, Illinois 60188. All rights reserved. The Living Bible, TLB, and The Living Bible logo are registered trademarks of Tyndale House Publishers.

Scripture quotations marked HCSB are taken from the Holman Christian Standard Bible®, Copyright © 1999, 2000, 2002, 2003, 2009 by Holman Bible Publishers. Used by permission. Holman Christian Standard Bible®, Holman CSB®, and HCSB® are federally registered trademarks of Holman Bible Publishers.

Scripture quotations marked NIRV taken from the Holy Bible, New International Reader's Version®. Copyright © 1996, 1998 Biblica. All rights reserved throughout the world. Used by permission of Biblica.

Scripture quotations marked ICB are taken from The Holy Bible, International Children's Bible® Copyright©

All for Jesus, Bob

1986, 1988, 1999, 2015 by Thomas Nelson. Used by permission.

Scripture quotations marked AMP are taken from the Amplified® Bible, Copyright © 2015 by The Lockman Foundation. Used by permission.

Scripture quotations marked AMPC are taken from the Amplified® Bible, Copyright © 1954, 1958, 1962, 1964, 1965, 1987 by The Lockman Foundation. Used by permission.

Made in the USA
Middletown, DE
22 January 2024